Fifty-Two

Weekly Reflections For

Cups of Coffee

The Contemplative Soul

Natalie Brown

Fifty-Two Cups of Coffee
Weekly Reflections for the Contemplative Soul
Copyright © 2018 Natalie A. Brown
ISBN 978-0-359-14533-1

Requests for information should be addressed to:
Natalie Brown
Website: www.natalieabrown.com
Email: nbcreative22@gmail.com

Cover Design + Cover Photography: Ireana Cook

For God –

This book has always been yours.

I will extol the Lord at all times;
his praise will always be on my lips.

Psalm 34:1 NIV

Table of Contents

Foreword

Huntley Brown

Speaking today into the lives of young people, who are inundated with so many different worldviews and cultural expressions, is never easy. God has gifted Natalie Brown in a unique way to address this changing generation.

Watching Natalie blossom into the incredible writer she is has been quite a journey. When she was just a young child, her mother and I called Natalie a mighty woman of God. We knew the Lord had an Esther-like plan for her, but we had no idea what that would look like. As she started to write, not only our family but also everyone who read her work realized God had anointed and appointed her for such a time as this.

These chapters are written from an honest place, addressing real-life issues with wisdom and tact. They are not one-time readings; they are packed with so much truth you will want to return to them again and again.

As you read, ask God to illuminate the different chapters for you, and I guarantee they will change your life.

A Note from the Author

To know me is to know my love for coffee shops. If I'm not at home, I'm probably at Starbucks and if I'm not at Starbucks, I'm probably at some other local café. It is at coffee shops, I've noticed, that I am my most authentic self. This is where I feel the most permission to let my guard down. Writing this book has felt like showing up for coffee 52 times. This is in part because I wrote quite a few of these reflections in various cafés, yet equally because with each word, phrase, and conjoining sentence, I released my need to be understood and simply began to share.

52 Cups of Coffee did not start out as a book. Rather, this story began as a single email which then turned into weekly emails now known as *Thursday Thoughts*, but we'll get to that. For now, you should know that I've spent the last year and a half thinking of you. I've re-written and edited some of my favorite *Thursday Thoughts* to create what you now hold in your hands.

What I found throughout the process, is that a great portion of the Gospel deals with storytelling. I see it most clearly in John chapter four as the Samaritan woman drops her water jar and runs to share of her encounter with the living Lord. Personally, I enjoy storytelling most with a fancy beverage in hand. So, here's an invitation – let's get coffee! Let's spend five minutes or an hour, or however long we need to sit, be still, and remember the goodness of God.

What you will find here is not a series of lessons, but a collection of stories. At the end of this book, my hope is not that you will have a greater understanding of who I am, but a deeper conviction to pursue the heart of God. With each reflection, I have included a prompt for your usage. I encourage you to use the blank pages provided to record your thoughts and spiritual insights.

As you read, may you be reminded of the beauty that surrounds you. As you reflect, may you be drawn towards the voice of God. And like a good cup of coffee on a long day, I pray these words reinvigorate you to see the world with renewed energy, focus, and passion.

Welcome to *52 Cups of Coffee!*

Natalie Brown

Part I.

Cup 1 | Exhale

"Therefore, since we are surrounded by such a great cloud of witnesses, let us throw off everything that hinders and the sin that so easily entangles. And let us run with perseverance the race marked out for us, fixing our eyes on Jesus, the pioneer and perfecter of faith."

Hebrews 12:1&2 NIV

If we're going to spend the next 52 weeks together, then we might as well get comfortable and start things off on a deeply honest note. I've never been good at this. I'm more of a *listener* than a *sharer*. I like to hide behind what's unsaid because you can't hold what you don't know against me. Well, not this time. If I'm going to be obedient to God and honoring to the vision placed on my heart, then I have to get really real with you. I believe this is where grace – the uncomplicated gift of redemption – bares its beautiful face. With that said, let's begin with the truth: I'm a recovering perfectionist. Which really means I am exceptionally hard on myself and have a difficult time letting things go. Choosing to write and share this collection of stories feels exceptionally personal and remarkably hopeful, and so, with both in hand, I want to tell you about one of the more embarrassing moments in my life: my first track meet.

The evening was loud and full of adrenaline. I was scheduled to run in the last women's event of the evening: the 4x4, and shortly before the race, I was assigned the role of anchor. If you are unfamiliar with track terminology, anchors are the last people to compete in the relay. It is their responsibility to pick up any slack and push forward towards victory. Needless to say, I was both honored and terrified.

As the race began, my team kept a steady pace, but we were still a considerable distance behind first place. I was fast — not exceptional, but decent, so I held a certain confidence that I could catch up and lead my team to victory. With a successful handoff from my partner, I took off onto the track with determination. With each stride, the distance between myself and the runner before me began to close. With each second, I pushed myself even harder. *I'm doing it!* I thought to myself. *I'm really doing it!*

With about 50 meters left in front of the first-place competitor and only a few seconds to go, I decided to leave nothing on the track and push myself as far as I could go. Though exceptionally tired and out of breath, I told myself that it was *mind over matter* and I could rest on the other side. This is where things got uncomfortable. Right as I planned to lunge forward gracefully into the next placeholder, it happened...In front of my friends, family, teammates, and a mélange of strangers, I fell. In a flashing moment, my legs scraped against the floor and my face hit the ground, ultimately disqualifying my team. My mom and track coach had to carry me, bringing my shame and embarrassment with me, off the field.

For weeks I cringed at the thought of the evening's event, questioning where and how I went wrong.

"Your legs gave out on you," was the response given to me by most. This much was obvious, but why?

A few weeks later, a close family friend who was present at the meet, recalled the event with me.

"I watched you as you rounded the corner," she said. "I noticed that you were holding your breath. 'Breathe, Natalie!'

I screamed from the top of the track, 'Breathe!' but you couldn't hear me."

There it was. In the midst of my quest to finish, I failed to remember the basic principles of running well. Consumed by the need to win, I discarded all ideas of practicality and personal capability and pushed myself to a place for which I had not trained. My body couldn't take it.

If I'm honest, I all too easily exhibit the same in my spiritual walk. In seasons of uncertainty – be it college applications, post-graduate jobs, first dates, financial concerns, etc. – the space between where I am and where I hope to be quickly becomes a fuzzy haze of striving, striving, and more striving. When I'm not careful, I begin to run with increased speed, holding my breath in anticipation for the end, rather than breathing deeply and running well throughout the process.

What I know now, though I must continuously remind myself, is that in Christ, we are given space to exhale. Romans 8:28 tells us that all things work together for good to them that love God and have been called according to God's purpose. This promise frees us from a standard of perfection and invites us into a life of discipline characterized by grace. Even in the midst of life's most pressing challenges, we can breathe deeply, for Christ is doing a work far beyond what we can see. This is not to say that we don't work hard or push ourselves to new levels, but rather that we do not have to carry the burdensome weight of perfection in order to finish well. And in a world where we are constantly thrown into various trials, turns, and races of our own, I believe it is of the essence that we become people who know how to enter the arena and finish well.

If I could go back to that night, my senior year, I'd tell the anxious, nervous, and ultimately hopeful girl before me to stop, breathe, and exhale. I hope you do the same.

- *Where in your life can you release yourself from the pressure of perfection?*
- *How can you trust God in this circumstance or situation instead?*

Cup 2 | Faithful in the Wait

"I remain confident of this: I will see the goodness of the Lord in the land of the living. Wait for the Lord; be strong and take heart and wait for the Lord."

Psalm 27:13-14 NIV

When I first moved to Washington, D.C., I was anxious to settle down quickly. On one occasion, I asked my friend, Stacy, for prayer, offering her a list of things I wanted God to provide. She responded with kindness and a bit of conviction as she told me,

"Yes, Natalie, I will pray for those things with you, and I'm also going to pray that you will be faithful in your wait."

Faithful in my wait? Her words exposed my apprehension to patience and challenged me to engage with my current season differently. Since then, I have often thought about this sentiment. Truth be told, I am not nearly as patient as I would like to be. And to be honest, patience, as it relates to matters more pressing than my immediate needs – like justice and peace, seems like an unaffordable luxury. Maybe this makes faithfulness all the more necessary. In reading Psalm 27, I have been reminded of the power of hope within our seasons of waiting. While waiting is unavoidably filled with a certain tension, hopeful waiting unearths greater expectancy. I am reminded of this every December.

At the heart of Advent lies a call for hopeful anticipation, yet I often wonder if we leave it there. As I read the Christmas story, I am reminded that Christ's birth did not bring about the initial change some might have expected. In fact, it's probable that on the night of Jesus' birth, life looked exactly the same.

Imagine that?

In one corner of the universe a divine miracle had occurred: *Emmanuel, God is with us at last!* The shepherds flocked, the angels sang, the wise men brought their offerings, and yet, I would imagine, in other places and spaces, life looked eerily familiar. As baby Jesus opened his eyes to the beautiful and broken world he loved enough to save, the people slept, they ate, they worked, they complained – all while earth, as it had been known, was completely altered. We are not always privy to the ways in which the ground is shifting beneath us. Sometimes change, and the faith to wait for it, requires deeper confidence and trust.

In my own life, I have noticed that Christ calls me towards deeper attention in my seasons of waiting. My default is to see all that is wrong or unfinished, yet when I take time to be still and listen, my eyes begin to notice all that is being redeemed. In turn, I am compelled to see life from a place of abundance rather than one of deficit. Christ's hope is not inactive; it is intentional, inviting us into a wild and wonderful journey along the way.

Time continues to teach me that God always shows up, most times within the unexpected, but each time with power, grace, and truth. To me, this type of divine intercession will always be worth the wait.

- *How is God calling you to be faithful in your wait today?*

Cup 3 | Gifts of Desperation

Luke 8:40-56

Where do you go when you're desperate?
Who do you become when all hope seems lost?

In her book, *Plan B: Further Thoughts on Faith*, Anne Lamott writes: "In my experience, there is a lot to be said for desperation – not exactly a bright side, but something expressed in words for which 'God' could be considered an acronym: Gifts of Desperation."

I wasn't sure what to make of this statement at first. God is so much bigger than an acronym centered on despair. With further contemplation, however, I have found something of deep value here, especially as it relates to the circumstances of Luke 8. Desperation in tandem with unrelenting faith is a preceding gift of transformation.

In Luke 8:40-56, desperation led a man of privilege and a woman considered an outcast into the arms of Christ. In both instances, desperation emptied these individuals of their capabilities and resources. In their emptiness, they, in turn, opened themselves to be filled with something they could not manufacture on their own. While the young ruler had the authority and hopeful audacity to plead before the people, the bleeding woman had the quiet resolve to go amongst them. And in front of the crowd, Jesus sees them both.

For years, I viewed this passage through the lens of the bleeding woman. Her story is a beautiful declaration of faith despite challenging circumstances. Recently, however, a friend invited me to see this narrative through the lens of Christ, offering that this story shows us a God who desires to be in the small moments with us – even when they don't seem small to us.

In the midst of desperate faith and trying circumstances, we find a God that sees before and beyond the moment of change, and there is a great deal offered along the way. The bleeding woman was not only healed but also given back her voice. The young leader was given more than resurrection, but an opportunity to journey with Christ. In this story, desperation was met with restoration. And isn't restoration the resounding cry of the gospel? As old is made new and wrong is made right, we are reminded to pay attention and participate. God is on the move and calls us to walk with Him. This walk of faith is one of renewal, though it often requires an understanding of our own desperation to get there.

So perhaps Anne Lamott is right, and our moments of desperation paired with our encounters with God lead us to find deeper transformation. Where desperate faith meets the power of hope, there is a Gift of Desperation.

So, where do you go when you're desperate?
Who do you become when all hope seems lost?

- *I encourage you to reflect on a specific encounter when desperation led you into the arms of Christ.*

Cup 4 | Transitional Spaces

"Yet the Lord longs to be gracious to you; therefore he will rise up to show you compassion. For the Lord is a God of justice. Blessed are all who wait for him!"

Isaiah 30:18 NIV

Birthdays have always been a magical day in the Brown household. It's the one day a year where everything is catered to one person. The morning begins with a lighthearted tradition as everyone (excluding the birthday individual) piles into the hallway. Then, with a unique pitch that can only be achieved at 6:45 am, they walk into the birthday person's room– gifts in hand – singing "Happy Birthday." As a child, there was nothing I loved more than the space of time that occurred as I pretended to be asleep and waited for my family to arrive. Amusingly, I've had very few other experiences where waiting has felt as joy-filled.

So much of the Bible deals with *waiting*. In Luke 1, Mary waits for the birth of her foretold son. In Exodus, the Israelites wait to reach the Promised Land. In Daniel 6, King Darius waits for Daniel to return from the lion's den. The Bible is filled with stories like these, and with each story, we are challenged to consider the notion of waiting well for the fulfillment of God's promises. With each promise, we are drawn to see that waiting is not a confident display of inaction, but a steady walk of expectancy.

I learned recently that in the Hebrew translation of the Bible, *hope* and *wait*, are often used interchangeably. I believe Mary (mother of Jesus) teaches us a lot about this concept. While Mary was given the promise of what was to come – the birth of a savior – she was not offered a guide for how the upcoming months would unfold. Though she was promised a great reward, she was first required to wait, and this waiting came with great sacrifice and a daily need to practice faith. Imagine the shame, confusion, and doubt that must have been directed towards Mary as she waited for her promise, yet even so she demonstrates unrelenting hope.

What I desperately want to learn from Mary is the ability to wait well. Though the journey ahead was long and hard, she chose to be exceedingly grateful. The transitional space between Mary's promise and her delivered savior was one of great patience and trust, and it is here, I find, that hope – true, unrelenting hope is born.

This life is full of transitional spaces, areas where we must exercise trust and discipline to believe in what is to come, even when we cannot see it. The tension that arises in these spaces can ultimately prove to be the foundational grounds for which our hope is built. As Mary demonstrates through the gospels, true hope in Christ is always worth the wait.

- *How are you being called to wait?*
- *How can you practice greater hope in the middle of your wait?*

Cup 5 | On Prayer

"And about the ninth hour Jesus cried out with a loud voice, saying, "Eli, Eli, lama sabachthani?" that is, "My God, My God, why have You forsaken Me?"

Matthew 27:46 NKJV

I learned to pray when I was three years old at the dinner table. For years (and even now) my family concluded every meal together with a reflection on scripture and a time of prayer. This is a privilege I did not always understand, and admittedly – during my adolescent years, I began to feel a certain sense of moral obligation when it came to this spiritual practice. Life has a funny way of leading us back to the things we once took for granted, and this was certainly my story with prayer.

Towards the end of high school – when the future felt so uncertain, my self-perception was weak, and the pressure to be seen, known, and understood was strong – I began to pray with more honesty. A deep sadness was slowly creeping in, in a way I could not control; but my belief in God kept me hopeful. In the process, I learned that prayer is both a posture and practice. As we draw ourselves towards stillness in God, we are reminded of His Divine power and our inherent identity as His children, a relationship that is truly sacred.

What I didn't know for many years is that prayer is not just a recurring act, but a way of *being*, and that every moment is suitable ground to participate. I used to believe we needed quiet spaces, empty journal pages, or even – at the very least – a bowed head and closed eyes, but now, I am slowly finding that prayer can manifest wherever we allow it.

I read recently that any situation can be used for prayer, including our joys, frustrations, and uncertainties, each one becoming a prayer when we present them to God. I love this idea, that God wants us to use any and every situation to come to Him and not our own flimsy means of survival. I am learning that prayer is not simply about finding a means to an end, or a wishing basket for all our desires, but rather it is entering a deeply transformative, healing, and beautiful conversation with God. One where we can be children in the arms of a parent – vulnerable, needy, curious, quiet, delightful, the whole thing.

People now tell me that I pray a lot, and this is true – it's the way I like to begin and end conversations. I pray frequently because I know that it works – if even not always in the ways that I had hoped. Furthermore, I pray expectantly because I have witnessed its sacred effect, continuously reminding all present: God is in our midst.

· *I encourage you to offer up an honest prayer on this page. Let it be messy, imperfect, and real. Trust that God is already waiting to meet you there.*

Cup 6 | There's Room

"Behold, I am doing a new thing; now it springs forth, do you not perceive it?
I will make a way in the wilderness and rivers in the desert."

Isaiah 43:19 ESV

Yesterday was a particularly dreary winter day; the downpour of rain was slow and monotonous. Strangely, the sun shone rather brightly the day before, offering small signs of springtime hope. Apparently, winter has room this year for both.

I tell my friends that I am an impatient perfectionist. By this, I mean that I often want things figured out yet lack the necessary patience to observe the process of change. This mindset leaves little room for duality. Amid my quest for perfection and what I deem *good enough*, I leave no space to observe the hard and necessary growth that must occur along the way.

Recently my friend Katie told me:

"Waiting for perfection in this life is like waiting for every day to smell like spring. It happens sometimes, in glimpses or whole days of shalom. And there are also foggy, sleepy, gross days like today. We can either accept the rain as part of life, or we can deny that it exists. But still the rain is there. It is totally the essence of human life."

This is a beautiful and hard truth from which we can learn. Life, in all its forms, is complex. It is beautiful and broken, delicate and fierce, difficult and joy-filled, but we must make room to observe both. In light of present pain, troubles, and loss, we are invited to see that there is still life, beauty, and grace.

Isaiah 43:19 tells us that God is doing a new thing. This verse provides beautiful imagery for new beginnings birthed within old circumstances, simultaneously declaring that old can make way for new and death can break grounds for renewed life. This is the hope we have in Jesus Christ!

Perhaps in our acknowledgment of the good and bad, we make room for something new to take up space. Just as winter offers many moments of sunshine and heat, rain and snow, we can allow ourselves the chance to observe the same. Beauty *and* brokenness. Discomfort *and* freedom. Fault *and* redemption. There is room for both.

· *How can you find beauty in a painful or difficult situation this week?*

Cup 7 | Open our Eyes

"I pray that the eyes of your heart may be enlightened in order that you may know the hope to which he has called you, the riches of his glorious inheritance in his holy people,"

Ephesians 1:18 NIV

When I was a student at Hope College, I found that there was always a quiet revolution that occurred amongst the student body around the first signs of spring, even if it was still technically winter. As soon as the temperature reached near 60 degrees Fahrenheit, the shorts came out, sandals slid on, and ice cream runs began. It was a beautiful phenomenon, almost as if the campus chose to silently declare – *we will see spring again.* And in a town where the winters are perpetually long and frigid, this reminder always felt quite necessary. Perhaps the same is no less true of our lives today.

There is nothing more seemingly sacred than the calm after the storm, breath after it has been withheld, light at the end of the tunnel, but sometimes it takes a second to get there. On good days this is frustrating; on bad days this is maddening. So, how do we seek the potential of spring when we are still caught in the middle of winter?

In Ephesians chapter one, Paul writes to the believers in Ephesus, proclaiming his hope in Christ and calling on them to seek the same. In verse 18 he offers a prayer that the eyes of this church would be opened to understand the hope to which they have been called in Christ. At the time of this letter, Paul was in prison, yet somewhere within he was able to find the resolve to proclaim a hope bigger than his circumstances. Through this letter, Paul reminds the Church that hope is not always found in what is right before us; and I believe there is something valuable that we can learn here. Though certain seasons may be long, weary, and tiresome, we have been promised rest, freedom, and redemption. Through the spiritual opening of our eyes and hearts, we, too, can find a hope outside our present circumstances.

Will we be people who trudge through the darkness failing to witness the light, or will we choose to be a community that decides to remember *though weeping may last for a night, joy comes in the morning.* Today, like Paul, I pray that God will open our hearts to the deeper hope we have been offered in Christ, for this is a truth that always offers new life.

- *How can you ask God to open your eyes this week to a deeper hope?*
- *Where in your life, have your eyes been opened (either past, present, or future) to the hope you have been offered in Christ?*

Cup 8 | Peace Be Still

Matthew 8:23-27

Matthew chapter eight is a wild ride. There is healing, audacious faith, question, and conviction, and right towards the end, there is a *storm*. This story begins with chaos, fear, and uncertainty. Shortly after leaving a crowd, the disciples follow Jesus into a boat. While out at sea they encounter a storm, but Jesus is fast asleep.

Life feels this way sometimes, doesn't it? Suddenly and with visceral force, the winds and waves of life come against us and God appears to be absent. And the crazy thing is, in this particular story, Jesus led the disciples to the storm.

"Then he got into the boat and his disciples followed him. Suddenly a furious storm came up on the lake, so that the waves swept over the boat. But Jesus was sleeping." v23-34 NIV

Surely Jesus — fully God and fully man —had the omniscience to foresee the storm approaching. Surely, he could have postponed their endeavor until later in the evening, so why didn't he? Maybe because there was something to be learned amid instability? I believe Jesus understood the realm of his power; more than that, I believe he had confidence in it — *perhaps* he was simply waiting for the disciples to do the same.

To truly know that Jesus was a storm calmer, the disciples first had to experience a storm. And this is where things get messy. No one has been promised a life free of pain or testing circumstances. In fact, we are promised the opposite: *In this world you will have trouble. But take heart! I have overcome the world (John 16:33).* Though we have not been promised a pain-free life, we have been promised the presence of God in any and every circumstance. With this being the case, I believe we can learn a thing or two from the disciples and the way they handled their storm encounter.

As the waves rampage around them and in the midst of their fear, the disciples run to Jesus and not to their own means of survival. In the middle of terror, they wake up the one they believe to be asleep, and despite their worry, Jesus responds:

"He replied, 'You of little faith, why are you so afraid?' Then he got up and rebuked the winds and the waves, and it was completely calm." v26

In an instant and with a single command, chaos turns to order, fear turns to faith, life halts, and brokenness becomes beautiful — all because Christ said so. What the disciples gained this day was invaluable. Through an encounter with despair, they were invited to experience a deeper realm of Christ's power. I believe the same is afforded us today.

This week I am reminded that Christ's power shows up even in our darkest moments, and it is here that we are transformed. Perhaps we would all do well to wake Christ up a bit more, not because he is unaware of our circumstances, but rather because we need to witness the authoritative nature of his voice: a sound even the wind and waves obey.

- *When was the last time you experienced a storm? What did you do? Who did you turn to? How did you respond?*
- *How can you wake God up amid your storm today?*

Cup 9 | Thursday Thoughts

"Where there is no vision, the people perish: but he that keepeth the law, happy is he."

Proverbs 29:18 KJV

I suppose I should tell you how all of this came to be. The emails. The journey. The book in your hands. I think we've finally reached that point in the conversation.

It was mid-January, the second semester of my junior year of college. For some reason or another, I was exceptionally down in the dumps. It might have been the bitter cold of Holland, Michigan, or the intensity through which my academic semester had begun, but something left me apathetic to the world around me. One evening, I called my mom in tears, explaining,

"I just don't feel excited about anything anymore. I feel sad most of the time and I don't know what to do."

My mom, in her wisdom, knew this situation was beyond what was occurring around me and tapped into what was going on spiritually. *

"You know, Natalie" she offered. "I think what you're dealing with is a loss of vision. Lately, Dad has been discussing Proverbs 29:18 which states, 'where there is no vision the people perish.' Why don't you offer up the space you're in to God and allow Him to speak to you and renew your vision?"

So, I did. For two weeks, I came to God in prayer and humility, asking what He could possibly have in store for my life. And you know what? He answered. I didn't have a Moses moment; there was no burning bush or audible proclamation, but I began to pay greater attention to the passions He had placed on my heart. At that time, this list included writing and women's ministry. Slowly, my vision was being renewed, so I prayed that God would show me how to live into it more fully.

During this time period, one of my favorite authors, Hannah Brencher, had a weekly email she sent out on Monday Mornings. These emails were pep talks for her readers, and I was obsessed.

One afternoon my friend, Katlyn, mentioned in passing that she wanted to talk about something that had been placed on her heart. Later that day she told me,

"You know, Natalie, you've been going through this melancholy season and I think you should use writing as a vehicle of hope. Maybe you could send out an email on a day of the week like Hannah Brencher."

"Really!?" I thought out loud. "I guess that could be really fun, but what day would I send them?"

"What about Thursdays?" she offered. "I think Thursdays could use a little love.'"

And so, *Thursday Thoughts* began, and what started as a weekly email quickly turned into a movement of hope – a call for me to look for God in the everyday moments of life and share those findings with others. Initially, these emails were small reflections I sent to a list of about 20 people, but over time, the list continued to grow, reaching a number of people along the way. Now, those very reflections have become the basis for the book you hold in your hands.

I've since learned that the things I dream for myself always prove to be too small in comparison to the vision God has for me. The older I get, the more I see how wonderful of a storyteller God is. In my moments of deepest despair, He has met me with renewed vision and deeper hope. And so, I am learning what it means to say "yes" to God and His plan and purpose for my life. It always makes all the difference.

PS: If you are struggling with your own sense of purpose, I encourage you to spend 21 days in prayer. Set aside a pre-set period of time each day to spend with God. Begin with thanksgiving – it is always the best place to start, and then, ask God to reveal who you have been created to be and how you can more fully live in your calling.

*I believe God works in both supernatural and natural ways, furthermore, I believe that counseling, medication, and therapy can be very good, healthy, and extremely beneficial practices. If you are personally dealing with something much deeper than a season of *down in the dumps*, I highly encourage you to open up to someone you trust and ask for help.

- *Where in your life do you want to say "yes" to God?*
- *How is God waiting for your "yes" today?*

Cup 10 | Declarative

Psalm 23

Psalm 23 continuously reminds me that I am not alone. More than that, it tells me I am seen, cared for, and protected. I've grown to see its message as a pressing form of declaration, an exclamation of who God is and what God can do in any and every circumstance.

I've started to begin the day speaking these words before I get out of bed, and it has become a grounding force for my life, a declaration that God is good, even amid adversity. I pray these words serve as a declarative reminder for you as well. We don't go alone; we go with Christ.

...

An adaptation of Psalm 23:

God, you are my leader, guide, caretaker, and friend.

In You I lack no good thing.

You bring me to places of life and rest, even amidst the chaos.

You restore my soul.

You direct me in the ways of Your Truth and I am transformed in the process.

Even though I go through treacherous times, I will not be afraid, for you are with me; your boundaries and guiding discipline protect me.

You overwhelm me with goodness even during adversity.

You call me your own and I am always satisfied.

I am confident that in you I lack no good thing, and to be in your presence is to be eternally grateful.

This is my hope. This is my prayer. This is my declaration.

· *I encourage you to write your own adaptation of Psalm 23 and declare it over yourself each morning this week.*

Cup 11 | Broken Dishes

"Create in me a pure heart, O God, and renew a steadfast spirit within me. Do not cast me from your presence or take your Holy Spirit from me. Restore to me the joy of your salvation and grant me a willing spirit, to sustain me."

Psalm 51:10-12 NIV

I am terrible at goodbyes, and it's not particularly the moment of release, but the way I handle the aftermath. Once, when I was younger, I spent the first 20 minutes of a 13-hour flight crying over the fact that I would miss my mom. I've been prone to hold onto the past, quietly longing for all that was good when it was still within reach. I've noticed that this type of living forces you into a certain funk, offering with it a list of *shoulds* and *can'ts*. You *should* have done this differently. You *can't* have this or that. It is quite maddening, and yet it does not feel all too atypical from the surrounding narrative of the world.

Oftentimes, change can resemble brokenness, forcing us to face the fact that very few things stay the same. People grow old, policies change, times passes, and we are left with pieces of the former all the while tasked with moving forward. It is an intricate tension.

So, *how then shall we live?* In a world where change is inevitable yet challenging, nonetheless, what do we do with the broken pieces found along the way?

A while back, a friend shared with me the story of a newlywed couple who vowed to never discard their broken dishes. Instead, they decided to transform the disheveled pieces by recreating them into something new, offering a metaphor of sorts: *things will crack and they will break, but we won't give up. We will continue to see the potential within each gift of life.*

Sin has a way of shattering things, but perhaps we can learn a thing or two from these newlyweds. By allowing ourselves the space to see things for what they could be and not solely what they have been, we afford ourselves an intricate kind of grace. And is this not the very grace offered to us in Christ? God entered a world that is and was wholly good, yet devastatingly broken with the weight of sin and shame, and He offered a solution. Through the life and death of His son, He provided an inconceivable amount of healing and resistance. By this grace, we have been afforded our own supernatural glue to tend to our lives.

Much like the depicted couple, I believe we must uncover the determination and patience to do the work of reconciliation – to see things not solely for what they were but have, in due time, the potential to be. This is hard and worthwhile, though I believe only time and experience can show us how. We must do the work of picking up all that has been scattered and begin the process of making things whole. Perhaps grace is the glue we extend when things no longer fit like they used to. Perhaps it is the prayers of thanks, forgiveness, resistance, and resilience we offer when things break. We must be willing to name our brokenness, both self-induced and others caused. Here, I believe, we will uncover a greater gift of hope.

- *Where in your life do you need God's healing?*
- *How can you intentionally let God in this week?*

Cup 12 | It Is Well

"When he had received the drink, Jesus said, 'It is finished.' With that, he bowed his head and gave up his spirit."

John 19:30 NIV

Recently, after attending a chapel that concluded with the old hymn, *It is Well*, I listened as a member present relayed his difficulty singing the words.

"How can we honestly sing 'it is well' when so much is not well?" he offered. His question exposed an Achilles heel for most people in the room. As people of faith, we are constantly in the middle of what seems like a great contradiction – as we proclaim a deep and true hope, we are called to face all that is seemingly without it.

Similarly, there is great paradox within Lent, found within our steady march towards death and rebirth. In this season we are given a rhythm of lament and celebration. As we walk through the gospels and towards the cross, we are reminded that we could not save ourselves. I see this dynamic tension on the night of Christ's crucifixion.

On the evening of his death and with his final breath Christ cried out, *"it is finished."* I have been thinking about the duality of this statement lately given its context. To many, those words must have seemed hopeless and symbolic of death, but in reality, they were a cry of hope and new life. In the midst of mockery, darkness, and despair Christ declares to us that it has been made well. God's present grace transcends our present circumstances and proclaims our present hope.

Despite all that would still need to be done here on earth, Christ asserts something unwavering. It is something we can build our life upon. God's mercy enters the pain with an unrelenting hope found in the celebration of Christ's impending resurrection. *You needed me, and I came*, it tells us.

In a world so noticeably tainted by its brokenness, we must remember this incomparable truth: it *is* finished! Lent brings us to a grounded place of rest in something much greater than ourselves. As we lament the brokenness before us, we can engage with relentless hope. As we aim to seek justice here on earth, we do so with the comfort of God's steady guidance. We can walk knowing we do not enter life's trials and circumstances alone. This does not make living in a broken world easy, but it does make it worthwhile.

It is finished! This is the hope we have this season, and because of it, I believe we can continue to say *it is well*.

- *There are many beautiful renditions of the old hymn "It Is Well." I encourage you to listen to one this week and give thanks for what God has done, is doing, and will continue to do.*

Cup 13 | Present Grace

"My grace is sufficient for you, for my power is made perfect in weakness."

2 Corinthians 12:7-9 ESV

I often find God most clearly within metaphors. Occasionally, a life circumstance or parallel that comes from it leads me to deeper reflection on the gospel. I like to think of these moments as windows of grace: spontaneous occurrences where I see or feel God through a specific event. It happened recently when I found an old note I had written tucked in a drawer in my room. I'd like to share it with you this week.

. . .

Remember the days you used to do it all, or at least try to?

You'd draw your own conclusions, forge your own pep talks, and create your own *best steps*.

And even with the best of intentions, you fell short.

Self-satisfaction has a way of doing that to us. We think we're just a little bit farther away from the *key*, then a little bit farther, and then a little bit farther, and often times we fail to realize we've been trapped by our own limitations. The rabbit chase is long, tricking us into missing its deceptive precepts – but not God's grace.

God's grace is sufficient. Present tense.

It's not the kind of thing you have to run for or chase after because it continuously meets you exactly where you are. This is what Christ's life, death, and resurrection promise: *present grace.*

And what an intricate gift this is proving to be.

. . .

I'm learning that God's grace gives us permission to be messy. In acknowledging that we can't do it all on our own, we make room for the one who can. Christ gave that to us – the chance to be completely empty and in turn find fullness in Him.

- *Where has the grace of God presented itself to you this week?*
- *Where do you feel you can't see it?*

Part II.

Cup 14 | Surprised in Eastertide

John 20:24-29

I learned recently that Easter is more than a day of commemoration, but a season of celebration. *Eastertide* is its official title — a period of days between the commemorative resurrection of Christ and the celebration of Pentecost. Shortly after, I was challenged by a co-worker to be surprised by God within this season. *Surprised in Eastside*, if you will. Since her initial call to notice, I have found a sense of surprise within the story of Thomas the disciple.

Within church settings, Thomas is often viewed through the lens of his unbelief. "Don't be a doubting Thomas," we say. If I'm honest, the story of Thomas used to frustrate me. Perplexed by his doubts in contrast with the weight of God's promise, I judged him.

Of course, resurrection is no small thing to understand, but Thomas had witnessed the strength of Jesus' power before, so why did he doubt that same power now?

With time and new insight, I have begun to read this story differently. Perhaps one's experience with resurrection is a lot more complex than I often choose to see, and maybe Thomas is more like me than I ever cared to believe.

In re-reading Thomas and the resurrection story, I now see things differently. While the disciples jumped on the *"new life in Christ"* bandwagon after witnessing the empty tomb, Thomas sat in his reservations.

Unless I see the nail marks in his hands and put my finger where the nails were, and put my hand into his side, I will not believe, he tells them.

But maybe the disciples approached Thomas in the midst of his mourning. Perhaps Thomas's doubts had less to do with a failure to believe in what had come to pass, and more to do with the weight of the trauma he had experienced. Over the course of just a few days, he witnessed the betrayal, rejection, and crucifixion of Jesus. This series of events is not for the faint of heart, and I wonder how often we find ourselves here — perhaps not as extreme, but caught within the depth of our own heartbreak, nonetheless.

It is hard to run to the promise of the resurrection when we are confronted by painful images of the past. When I sit in this story, I find a man who has met his limits. Restrained by the weight of his own doubt, Thomas had no option left but to wait for something or someone greater than the realm of his experience. It is here that hope is born.

As the chapter continues: *"Though the doors were locked, Jesus came and stood among them and said, 'Peace be with you!'"*

As Thomas sits in the weight of his own understanding, Jesus shows up. Amid his doubt, hurt, pain, and longing, Christ appears, revealing the scars of resurrection and the joys of hope. When Thomas has nothing to bring to the table: no hope, no faith, no belief, Christ reveals himself — even with locked doors — and calls him into belief. How might God be doing the same for you today?

- *How have you been surprised in Eastertide?*
- *When has God shown up in your life when the doors were "locked" and offered you hope?*

Cup 15 | Rhythms of Grace

"Are you tired? Worn out? Burned out on religion? Come to me. Get away with me and you'll recover your life. I'll show you how to take a real rest. Walk with me and work with me—watch how I do it. Learn the unforced rhythms of grace. I won't lay anything heavy or ill-fitting on you. Keep company with me and you'll learn to live freely and lightly."

Matthew 11:28-30 MSG

I believe there are two types of people in this world: those who were born to dance, and those who will spend their life trying. I've come to accept the fact that I belong in the latter category. Yep, that's me...the person in the background hoping she can get by with a simple two-step. There is nothing profound about this information, except that it should help you visualize what it was like for me to take an African Dance class my senior year of college.

Life has a funny way of working within the unexpected, and what I thought would be a small step outside of my comfort zone quickly proved to be a recurring chance to learn more about God's faithful promise of grace.

African Dance tells a story. It is not the coming together of singular movements, but an unfolding tale of what is and what has been, ultimately creating something extremely raw and beautiful.

This style of dance is full of vibrant movements that appear effortless yet require a deep sort of mental dedication. There's a stream of consciousness that occurs as the beat of the drum aligns with the unfolding dance movements, and this is where I often got stuck.

Amid our various routines, I was quick to ponder what came next and how I was supposed to adjust my position once the current move ended. In the midst of my analyzation, I often missed the beauty of the beat.

Throughout this dance class, I noticed an uncomfortable familiarity with the ways my spiritual life was aligning with my dance life. In both scenarios, I was always trying to rush ahead, figure things out on my own, and be one step ahead of the instructor. This way, I assumed, I would never be caught off guard by the unexpected details or movements. As you can imagine, this not only makes way for clumsy routines, but a clumsy and uncomfortable life.

I told a friend about my spiritual dilemma and in response, she shared wisdom rooted in Matthew 11:28-30.

"God wants to take your burdens from you so that you can find contentment and perfection in Him and not your own capabilities," she offered.

God spoke to me deeply through her words. What I failed to see in my spiritual life, and dance class, is that while both require a necessary discipline, grace gives us room to live with freedom. In listening to the beat and leaning into the movements at hand, we can learn the unforced rhythms of grace. Faith is not about mastering life, and it's not a code of conduct filled with rules and regulations. As Jesus promises in Matthew 11, grace offers us a step-by-step sort of faith walk. In placing Jesus' yoke upon ourselves, we are given room to live *freely* and *lightly*, learning God's ways as they become our own.

- *How can you let go and let God this week?*
- *Where can you pay attention to rhythms of grace this week?*

Cup 16 | Meet Me at the Well

John 4: 1-45

What I find to be most fascinating about the life and ministry of Jesus, is the way he is always doing what should not be done in the eyes of the world, but perfectly right in the Kingdom of God. John chapter four – the story of the Samaritan woman – is my favorite example. With a single question, and to a woman he *should* have had no business talking to, Jesus obliterates several gendered, cultural, and social prejudices while demonstrating the heart of the gospel: Christ came for all.

As readers, we are invited into a story of belonging, but first, we are introduced to the margins. Theologians have said that given the racial class and social standing of Samaritans at this time, it is more than likely that the woman in this story was an outcast. This is most likely why she arrived at the well at the sixth hour (around noon), for this was resting time – thereby making the area deserted. Condemned by her past and cultural identity, she was forced to hide within the shadows. Jesus, however, cares far less about what others have to say about her, and much more about whom He knows her to be: a daughter of God. Despite her social inconveniences and past history, Christ calls her worthy.

There is much to glean from this story, but today I am captivated by the space in which it takes place. This is our first account of Jesus revealing his divine identity and he chooses to do it at a watering station. If I were Jesus, I might have chosen something a little more dramatic such as a dinner party or large body of water. But no, Jesus chooses a well: a commoner's place. Jesus takes a daily occurrence and transforms it into something sacred.

Suddenly, the well is no longer a singular destination for daily fulfillment, but a conversion point, a physical reminder of the power of God transforming our ordinary spaces into testimonies of His love. What I love about this story is its intrinsic reminder that God turns our ordinary moments into extraordinary experiences. With a single touch from Christ, that which is mundane becomes transformative and holy.

And so, I can't help but wonder: what are our *well* moments? What are the places we show up to out of necessity, yet simultaneously the spaces where we don't always feel that we belong? Perhaps it is in these very spaces that Christ meets us most clearly, drawing us to see His divine identity and asking us to name it as such. Just like the woman at the well, Jesus tells us that we are worthy of the Gospel message and furthermore fully qualified messengers of its worth.

So, how might God be trying to meet you at the well today?

- *Where in your life do you feel like the outcast and how has God met you there?*
- *How has God taken an ordinary moment in your story and turned it into something extraordinary?*

Cup 17 | All the Light

"Shout for joy to the Lord, all the earth. Worship the Lord with gladness; come before him with joyful songs. Know that the Lord is God. It is he who made us, and we are his; we are his people, the sheep of his pasture."

Psalm 100:1-3 NIV

Last weekend I accompanied my sister on a babysitting gig. The evening was filled with Star Wars, dress up, and many artistic paintings. When it was time for bed, the kids gathered around the bedroom table to say their nightly prayer. As we bowed our heads and closed our eyes one child began:

"Dear God, thank you for the polar bears on my pajamas and thank you that my baby sister has stopped crying. Amen."

Short, sweet, and filled with gratitude. I sat there and wondered why I don't do the same. Why don't I give more thanks for the simple things, like the chuckle my dad makes that sounds exactly like my Grandmother's, or Trader Joe's ice cream, or the gray scarf that keeps me warm all winter? This is the light I fail to see.

All too often I center my attention on what needs fixing and how it became so broken. It's all too easy to give focus to the darkness because oftentimes the darkness feels so much more apparent. Death and grief are not silent entities; neither is injustice or prejudice – but neither is hope or redemption.

In the gospel of Luke, after Mary is given news that she is with child, she runs to her cousin Elizabeth who responds with exclamation,

---

"Blessed are you among women, and blessed is the child you will bear! ... As soon as the sound of your greeting reached my ears, the baby in my womb leaped for joy. Blessed is she who has believed that the Lord would fulfill his promises to her!"' Though the hope Mary carried was still inside, Elizabeth gave thanks in the present. I want to do the same.

In the midst of my worries, fears, and insecurities, I am working on choosing to see the light. And while I believe there is only one *true* source of light in this world, last week, a 3-year-old reminded me that this light can prove itself in both quiet and triumphant ways. Perhaps the art of noticing, is its own act of thanksgiving, ultimately giving way to greater hope.

I hope you find the undeniable light in your life this week as well.

- *I encourage you to write down five things you are grateful for every day this week.*

Cup 18 | A Story

"And I pray that you, being rooted and established in love, may have power, together with all the Lord's holy people, to grasp how wide and long and high and deep is the love of Christ, and to know this love that surpasses knowledge – that you may be filled to the measure of all the fullness of God."

Ephesians 3:17-19 NIV

The story below spilled out of me one afternoon during a season of intense transitions. I had recently returned from Cape Town, South Africa and was feeling the external pressure of transitions as I prepared for life after college. On this afternoon, my internal anxieties dismantled themselves into words on a page. God met me there. I pray you find God here too.

. . .

She began to feel the weight of change, once again, realizing that her life was always evolving and *stand still* moments were very few and far between. She was not active enough to resonate deeply with a mountain metaphor, but words on a page – that she could grasp. And soon she discovered that the Author of her life was continuously writing, continuously creating the character he had made her to be. She wanted to know this character. She truly did. But deep down, she longed to know the Author more. Perhaps within His identity, soul, and attention to detail, she could further understand the ways He had crafted her into a protagonist.

But alas, all too often she became distracted, focusing on what would come next and what had been left behind. Her desire to understand became ferocious, leaving its mark with frequently underlined words and dog-eared pages, constantly bringing her back to where she left off.

But her Author continued, using His intentional craft to create something beautiful in the present. Why couldn't she see that?

Maybe it was because she desired to write the story herself. She had a vision for her pages, yet all too often this Author seemed off track. Maybe it was that she was too consumed with the stories of others, forcing her to miss important parts of her own – periods she assumed to be commas, facts she read as satire, recounts of love she believed to be sarcasm. She missed some things in the quest for her own knowledge, but He, in a manner both kind and graceful, continued to write, repeating stories with new characters and underlining words of His own.

She still got distracted, so every now and then He'd close another chapter, gently forcing her to pay attention to the one before her. And He kept writing and writing and writing in hopes of the day she'd become so focused that all she would want to do was hear what He had to say.

It took time, but He finally got her attention, and once He did, the stories He had been telling all along became the vehicle through which she saw His love.

- *Where do you find yourself in the story God is writing?*
- *How are you responding?*

Cup 19 | Weeping

"Those who sow in tears shall reap with shouts of joy!"

Psalm 126:5 ESV

A ndy was everything I hoped to be when I got older. She was funny, kind, smart, and adventurous. She was the type of person who made life seem like something to be chased. And chase it, she did. To this day, Andy continues to teach me a great deal about courage, faith, and hope, even though she is no longer here to teach me these things herself.

My first experience with loss occurred a little over ten years ago when Andy was killed in a car accident. Only twelve at the time, I was quickly forced to confront the evil of death as Andy – my 24-year old basketball coach, music teacher, and all-around older friend – was taken without forewarning. To this day, it still feels quite unfair.

What do you do with this? What happens when life feels cruel, and hope seems more distant than not. Where do you go when life throws a loaded punch and all you can do is question the presence of God?

I'm sure there are profound theological answers to these questions; answers worth seeking and studying – but today, I do not have those answers to share. Instead, I have a small pocket of hope found in the words of Psalm 126.

"When the Lord restored the fortunes of Zion, we were like those who dreamed. Our mouths were filled with laughter, our tongues with songs of joy. Then it was said among the nations, 'The Lord has done great things for them.'

The Lord has done great things for us, and we are filled with joy. Restore our fortunes, Lord, like streams in the Negev. Those who sow with tears will reap with songs of joy. Those who go out weeping, carrying seed to sow, will return with songs of joy, carrying sheaves with them." NIV

This Psalm is an honest lament before God. It is a decree of thanksgiving for what He has done before, and a desperate plea to see His goodness again. There is deep beauty left for us in this message, a true hope we can cling to in order to face the days ahead. While this passage holds the tension of mourning, it does so with the confidence of hope. It reminds us that though we weep, we can rest assured that we will not always be weeping. Though we mourn, we can trust that there is a day coming when we will mourn no more. Every wrong will be made right and every tear will be wiped from our eyes. This type of hope can only be found in Christ's life, death, and resurrection. It invites us to see the reality of a world devastatingly marked by pain, yet it doesn't leave us there. "Those who sow in tears shall reap with shouts of joy!" I often go back to this promise when I think about Andy.

This life we have been given comes with a great deal of reward and responsibility. Though inherently beautiful and full, it is not devoid of pain or challenge. Like anything worthwhile, we must give ourselves permission to see things as they are *and* as we hope them to be. And in matters of grief, I believe we can weep while we wait for the hope of tomorrow. But we must do so with a promise: *though we may sow with tear-stained eyes, we will harvest with great joy.*

- *How does Psalm 126 comfort you?*
- *How does it challenge you?*

Cup 20 | Touching Heaven

"Taste and see that the Lord is good;
blessed is the one who takes refuge in him."

Psalm 34:8 NIV

I wish I could take you to *That Place* – a small bookstore/coffee shop on Lower Main Road in Cape Town (yes, the name of the café is really *That Place*; South Africa is whimsical like that). I'd grab us a seat by the window and convince you to order the carrot cake. During my semester abroad, I'd frequent this café for coffee dates and study sessions. My friends and I would often joke that you go to *That Place* for the aesthetic and stay for the cake. It's just that good. I could go on and on, but you'd only know so much. The experience of taste versus the idea of it are two entirely different things. You know this, of course, so why do we often allow talk of God to supersede experience with God?

I've spent the better part of this week contemplating Psalm 34:8: "*Oh, taste and see that the Lord is good!*" At its core, this verse offers us a model for intentional observation, an anthem far more about experience than ideation. Here we are called to experience the reality of God's character rather than merely think or speak on it. With this in mind, I have been drawn to recall the promises of God and the ways I have witnessed their power. Here are just a few of my favorites:

- The Lord is near to the brokenhearted and saves those crushed in spirit. (Psalm 34:18)

- Even though I walk through the darkest valley, I will fear no evil, for you are with me. (Psalm 23:4)
- For the Lord God is a sun and shield; the Lord bestows favor and honor. No good thing does he withhold from those who walk uprightly. (Psalm 84:11)
- And we know that for those who love God all things work together for good, for those who are called according to his purpose. (Romans 8:28)

According to Bible Gateway, there are over 5,000 promises in the Bible. These verses are not solely concepts to consider, they are truths waiting for activation. When my dad was rushed to the emergency room, I witnessed the character of God displayed through the kindness of neighbors who dropped everything to drive me to the hospital. When I didn't know how I was going to pay for my first year of college, I experienced the generosity of a stranger through a $4,000 check given on a whim. When my laptop stopped working in the middle of writing *52 Cups of Coffee*, I watched God rally together a community who surprised me with a new one. These are personal examples, noticeably, but I believe that's partially the point. To truly know the goodness of God, we must take the time to witness it for ourselves. We must quiet the noise that tells us of all that is wrong and look for the grace manifested regardless.

Perhaps tasting the goodness of God is far less about suspended breath for better days and infinitely more about God's goodness within the day-to-day. The good news is that Heaven is breaking in here and now, but we must be willing to look, hear, and taste its effect. And when I choose to open my eyes, I see it – heard within genuine laughter and good-natured conversations. I find it within moments of uncommon courage and feel it within extensions of grace. Yes, with this type of living I am continuously drawn to see – when I stop to touch Heaven, I find Heaven is already touching me.

- *How has Heaven touched you lately?*
- *How can you reach out this week and intentionally seek the goodness of God?*

Cup 21 | On the Way

"The LORD had said to Abram, 'Go from your country, your people and your father's household to the land I will show you. I will make you into a great nation, and I will bless you; I will make your name great, and you will be a blessing.'"

Genesis 12:1-2 NIV

W hen I was living in Washington, D.C., people would often ask me, "What is your favorite thing about the city?", to which I would tell them: the *96* – a metropolitan bus route.

I felt a strange sense of apprehension each time I said it because surely it should have been the museums, or the people, or the diverse selection of food, or something – anything a bit more exciting than public transit. But alas, infatuated with the 96 is where I was.

On a typical weekday I'd hop onto this bus and make my way to work. The commute, while only 40 minutes in length, offered a great deal of conventional chaos along the way. There were laughing babies, upbeat school kids, cranky adults, and a medley of individuals passing the time. And with each expression of kindness, irritation, and resolve, a deeper sense of common humanity was felt. While our stories remained unbeknownst to each other, we sat well aware that we were all on our way to *somewhere*. For the allotted period, we were drawn towards each other, despite a world that continuously tried to pull us away. For this, I stayed continuously intrigued by the *96*.

A writer I admire once published an essay on movement. Her words proposed the idea that life, in all of its forms, requires a certain sense of perpetual motion, and with that motion lies the foundation of change. The older I get, the more I find this to be true.

In ancient history, travelers could take days, weeks, months, and even years to make the trek between their points of passage, thereby making the journey just as important as the destination. Truth be told, I've spent a lot of time confusing this idea, caring far less about the process and exponentially more about the arrival. In the midst of this mindset, I am quick to forget that things take time and grace to change. I fail to acknowledge that life is a marathon and not a sprint. Maybe this is why we are so easily tired. We constantly sprint a race meant to be jogged with pace, resilience, and perpetual motion.

This life of faith is not one of point-to-point destinations or revelations. Rather, it is a continuous journey requiring presence. When we show up with faithful expectation, we are drawn to see how God meets us with every step. It is this notion of perpetual movement that greets me on the bus each morning. As I sit and observe the complexity before me, I am reminded that life is a journey – one that should be noticed and maybe even noted. We are all on our way to something, and I have hope that this something is worth the wait.

- *What are you on the way to?*
- *Where do you feel God's leading to begin a new journey?*

Cup 22 | Prayer of Patience

"Trust in the Lord with all your heart, and do not lean on your own understanding. In all your ways acknowledge him, and he will make straight your paths."

Proverbs 3:5-6 ESV

Towards the beginning of my time in South Africa, I told my friend, John Luke, that I was having a difficult time being present. In response, he told me about Pierre Teilhard de Chardin (a Jesuit priest and philosopher) and his well-known prayer, *Patient Trust*. I'm not sure John Luke knew it at the time, but this quote proved to be everything I needed in the space I was in. I pray it's just as encouraging for you.

. . .

Patient Trust
Above all, trust in the slow work of God.
We are quite naturally impatient in everything
to reach the end without delay.
We should like to skip the intermediate stages.
We are impatient of being on the way to something
unknown, something new.
And yet it is the law of all progress
that it is made by passing through
some stages of instability—
and that it may take a very long time.
And so I think it is with you;
your ideas mature gradually—let them grow,
let them shape themselves, without undue haste.

Don't try to force them on,
as though you could be today what time
(that is to say, grace and circumstances
acting on your own good will)
will make of you tomorrow.
Only God could say what this new spirit
gradually forming within you will be.
Give Our Lord the benefit of believing
that his hand is leading you,
and accept the anxiety of feeling yourself
in suspense and incomplete.
>   —Pierre Teilhard de Chardin, SJ
>   (1881-1955, public domain)

· *What sticks out to you from this prayer?*
· *How is God trying to capture your attention today?*

Cup 23 | The Unfinished Story

"You have said, 'Seek my face.' My heart says to you, 'Your face, Lord, do I seek.'"

Psalm 27:8 ESV

I remember discussing the potential of New York City with my friend Katie just weeks before the start of her internship. She had plans to spend the summer learning and serving at a local church in Roosevelt Island, so we spent a fair amount of time thinking, praying, and preparing for her departure.

On one occasion, we sat in the cafeteria on a cool spring evening and contemplated her impending adventure – the people she'd meet, work she'd pursue, and experiences she'd have along the way. And while we did not romanticize the potential of this experience, there was undoubtedly a hopeful madness to it all. In this moment, New York was her unfinished story.

Life often feels like an unfinished story. As we live in the complexity of *now* and *not yet* we are forced to reconcile the notion that the answers are not always before us. Recently, I listened to a speech on courage, in which the speaker posed the question:

"How does your thinking change when you realize no one in the Bible knew how their story was going to end?"

The audience was invited to contemplate several Biblical figures who, at the time, were just another soul called upon by God.

Moses: an insecure and reluctant leader. Mary: a pregnant virgin and subsequent outcast. Jonah: a disobedient prophet. Esther: a young

Jewish orphan. Unfinished, these stories offer a great deal of tension, but they do not offer the end result. We no longer characterize these individuals by who they once were, but rather by who they became in obedience to Christ.

Moses: a leader of liberation. Mary: mother of the Savior and witness to the resurrection. Jonah: declarer of God's righteousness. Esther: Queen of Persia and advocate of hope. A constant theme is found here: *God is always faithful and calls us to be the same.*

. . .

A few weeks before I moved to Washington, D.C. and two weeks before Katie finished her time in New York, I hopped on a plane and went to visit her. As I prepared to venture into the start of my own unfinished story, I was able to witness the completion of hers. While NY was beautiful and charming, I left with far more than mere pictures or a travel experience; rather I was offered a certain hope. I returned with a story of God's faithfulness; a reminder that He meets us within the unfinished and crafts a story of love, redemption, hope, and faith along the way. Witnessing the unfolding of Katie's unfinished story gave me greater confidence, humility, and trust to enter my own. And this, I believe, is the particular blessing and power of each of our stories today.

Deeper faith lies at the heart of the unfinished story, for it is here that God meets us in divine and transformative ways. As we trek through the unknown, we are drawn to see that we do not walk alone. Christ goes with us.

And so, in a world that continues to feel so much like that of an unfinished story, my prayer is that you continuously find the strength to keep reading. We know how *this* story ends, and that is a hope worth proclaiming.

- *Where do you see an unfinished story within your life today?*
- *What scripture can you proclaim throughout your journey?*

Cup 24 | Simply Showing Up

"I sought the Lord, and he answered me and delivered me from all my fears.
Those who look to him are radiant, and their faces shall never be ashamed."

Psalm 34:4-5 ESV

I have always loved the book of Ruth, for it consistently points me back to the faithfulness of God. In this story, we are drawn to consider the reality of heartbreak, the prospect of redemption, and the value of community. Though Ruth is often painted as the protagonist, most recently, I have been compelled to consider the life and plight of Naomi. In many ways, I believe her story quite beautifully resembles our own.

The scene begins with loss and desperation. Naomi, who once was a woman full of faith, is now marked by her pain. *"Don't call me Naomi,"* she tells her community. *"Call me Mara, because the Almighty has made my life very bitter. I went away full, but the Lord has brought me back empty." (Ruth 1:20* NIV*)*

I feel for Naomi in ways I don't quite understand. Her relationship with loss seems to symbolize a world marked by the pain of its brokenness. In her despair, she declares her longing and uncertainty, *"I went away full, but the Lord has brought me back empty."* Can we be bold enough to acknowledge that sometimes we feel the same?

As the story continues, we are taken on a journey of love, hope, and redemption. As Ruth extends friendship to Naomi, God displays the radical ways He works within community. It's easy to look at the text and see Ruth as the hero (or even Boaz), but the real victor of the story is God. Through the faithfulness of His people, He reveals His divine plan of redemption, and as we read, we are invited to witness the beauty of simply showing up.

As the story goes, Boaz and Ruth later give birth to Obed who fathered Jesse who fathered David who is the line through which Jesus Christ was born, thereby making Naomi a great, great, great, great, great (you get the picture) grandmother to the coming Messiah. What began as a story of loss and despair ultimately transformed into one of hope.

"The town women said to Naomi, 'Blessed be God! He didn't leave you without family to carry on your life. May this baby grow up to be famous in Israel! He'll make you young again! He'll take care of you in old age. And this daughter-in-law who has brought him into the world and loves you so much, why, she's worth more to you than seven sons!'"
(Ruth 4:14&15 MSG)

The story of Ruth is a story of faithfulness. It is a fascinating recount of the power of presence in the presence of God. I encourage you to read through the book of Ruth this week. May you find that Naomi's story is our story and when we show up, we continuously find that God is already there.

- *What captivates your attention about the story of Naomi/Ruth/Boaz?*
- *How did the faithfulness of God present itself to you last week/last month/last year?*

Cup 25 | A Valley of Our Own

*"Then he said to me, 'Son of man, these bones are the whole house of Israel.
Behold, they say, 'Our bones are dried up, and our hope is lost; we are indeed cut
off.' Therefore prophesy to them...Then you shall know that I am the Lord; I
have spoken and I will do it, declares the Lord."*

Ezekiel 37:11-14 ESV

A few months ago, my family faced an unprecedented amount of trials. From the death of friends and family to emergency room visits and a fraudulent check, we were left perplexed and slightly disturbed by all that had gone so terribly wrong. I've since been reminded that sometimes life takes us to the valley, forcing us to face the ruins of a broken world. In these moments, it is always best to ask God what He wants us to see.

In Ezekiel 37, God leads the prophet Ezekiel to a valley of dry bones through a vision. Throughout the vision, God instructs him to wander back and forth, drawing his attention to all that is broken, dead, and dry. This has always been rather peculiar to me. Why would the author of life lead his servant to a passage of death?

After some time, God asks him,

"Son of man, can these bones live?" (Ezekiel 37:3)

I find it interesting how God tests Ezekiel's faith in this way, as if to say, *will you face ruin and still believe in my strength?*

Ezekiel answers in confidence,

"O Sovereign Lord, you alone know." Or, as the *Message* puts it, "Master God, only you know that." Here, Ezekiel stares despair head on and responds with a hope outside of himself, and as a result, God commands him to respond to what he has seen.

"Prophesy over these bones, and say to them, O dry bones, hear the word of the Lord…" (v4)

Through the power of the word of God, Ezekiel is commanded to speak to impossible situations with the hope of Christ, and through this prophecy, there is new life.

"And behold, a rattling, and the bones came together, bone to its bone. And I looked, and behold there were sinews on them, and flesh had come upon them, and skin had covered them….and the breath came into them and they lived and stood on their feet, an exceedingly great army." (v7-10)

Out of death, despair, and destruction, God births an army, and he does it through human participation. I am both challenged and encouraged by this idea, for it compels me to face my valley experiences differently. Perhaps God is asking us the same question he asked Ezekiel.

Child of God, can these bones live?

All too often it can feel as though we have been led to the valley. The bones of this day are massive and brittle. We are surrounded by stories of tragedy, injustice, death, and destruction. Yet, as this story reminds us, God is not terrified, and He does not expect us to be either. Though life may lead us to the valley, God reminds us that He is always there, oftentimes calling us to speak to our situations of despair and command new life through the name of our Lord.

So, child of God, do you believe old can be made new and death can offer new life?

May our response always be, "Oh Lord God, with you all things are possible."

- *Where in your life, do you feel you've been led to the valley?*
- *How is God calling you to respond?*

Cup 26 | The Open Door: A Short Story

"But he said to me, 'My grace is sufficient for you, for my power is made perfect in weakness.' Therefore I will boast all the more gladly of my weaknesses, so that the power of Christ may rest upon me."

2 Corinthians 12:9 ESV

The door marked boldly with *perfection* closed gently yet made its resounding cry nonetheless. It was a pesky thing, constantly creaking as it opened every now and then, filling her with silent hopes that she could be let in. But alas, it always closed, sometimes with a slam and other times with a gentle push. Today was one of those days. And so, she was faced with a choice. She could wait outside, anxiously wondering when the door towards perfection might open next. Or, she could choose to enter a different door, one whose hinges had been completely removed, leaving its entrance wide open. She always felt better, freer, once she got closer to this door; but it was the walking inside part that scared her. See, to go through this open door she first had to acknowledge that she could not get in through the other door. And she was silently ashamed.

The hallway, where she remained, was rather lonely, as no one spoke to each other. Some ran to the door of perfection, pounding loudly on its surface.

"Let me in!" they'd scream.

Others sat in silence, their hands folded as they mouthed, *"please, please, please, please."* And still, others stood tall, their faces expressionless as if they were unsure as to why they were outside in the first place. Through it all, the other door was always open, so why didn't they go inside?

And just as she began to consider the weight of her own complacency, it happened, just as it always does – someone stepped inside the open room. He had a familiar sorrowful face, for he had been sitting in the hallway for a while; but upon his entrance into the open room, his entire demeanor changed. He turned back to those within the hallway and smiled – an expression no one had seen for quite some time. As the tears began to roll down his face he exclaimed, *"This is where I belong."*

Intrigued by his appearance and captivated by whatever this room had to offer, she too made her way to the open door, but before stepping inside she took a moment to observe the words staring back at her on the doorstep mat: *Welcome to grace. We're glad you're here!*

- *What sticks out to you from this story?*
- *Where do you find yourself within it?*

Part III.

Cup 27 | Out of the Boat

Matthew 14:22-33

I'd like to think that if Peter and I were alive in the same time period, we'd either be the best of friends or worst of enemies. Peter and I are stubborn in similar ways. We are quick to jump to conclusions and slow to grasp the major point; yet even so, I believe our hearts beat to the same tune: we desire to truly follow the footsteps of Christ. Matthew 14 is no exception.

In this passage Peter tests the envelope and seeks deeper faith. Jesus did not ask Peter, nor any of the other disciples, to get out of the boat and come to him – but maybe just maybe Peter was so captivated by an unshakeable desire to be closer to Jesus that he faced his fears of moving beyond the shore.

There's a well circulated song by Hillsong United that talks about this very moment. The lyrics state: *"Spirit lead me where my trust is without borders. Let me walk upon the waters, wherever you would call me. Take me deeper than my feet could ever wander, and my faith will be made stronger in the presence of my savior."*

I remember singing this song one evening my freshman year of college and completely freezing, "Do I really want this?" I thought to myself. "Do I really want God to take me to a place where I can do nothing but trust Him?" These lyrics take on new meaning when we pause to reflect on what we are actually saying, so at the time, I decided to stop singing them. But Peter ... well, these lyrics are the cry of his heart and so he boldly asks for it: "Lord, if it's you, tell me to come to you on the water."

So, Jesus responds: "Come."

And isn't this amazing – sometimes Jesus just says "come." There's no - *grab a lifejacket* or *watch out for the impending waves on your left* or *make sure the boats follows closely behind you just in case*. No, Jesus simply says "come". And what a testament to His character and the divine authoritative nature of His presence. Jesus knows that He is enough to enable Peter to walk on water *and* lift him when he doubts.

The thing about getting out of the boat is that it requires us to trust in something bigger than our own understanding of the life we have lived thus far. To walk on water is to accept the notion that faith and Jesus transcend the realm of our natural understanding. To step out of the boat is to submit to the Lordship of Christ, rather than serve under the life precepts we have maintained for ourselves.

What Peter teaches me in this story is that it is worth it to get out of the boat for Jesus. Though Peter was tossed by the waves at hand, Christ was strong enough to save him and reassure him that God is bigger than the wind and waves of this life.

What I failed to allow to take root that evening my freshman year of college is the weight of the words behind the desperate act: *"Take me deeper than my feet could ever wander, and my faith will be made stronger in the presence of my savior."*

By stepping outside of the realm of our own *power* we open ourselves up to something much deeper. We invite the presence of God to transform our hearts and re-establish our confidence in something that lasts. Though I'd like to think that the faith of all the disciples was strengthened this evening, only Peter was able to return to the boat with "Hey, this Jesus guy walks on water, and when I keep my eyes on him, I do too."

- *How might God be calling you to get out of your own boat today?*
- *Where has God met you despite your discomfort before, and how might He be calling you to do so again?*

Cup 28 | Enough for Today

"When you have Christ, you are complete. He is the head over all leaders and powers."

Colossians 2:10 NLV

My agenda yesterday evening was simple: *hop off the bus* (at the correct stop this time), *walk down 14th street, purchase sour cream, refrain from purchasing dried mango, walk home.* Life, however, had other plans.

As I made my way off the crowded bus and onto the side street, a slow tugging began to occur on the left side of my body. I glanced at my shoulder only to discover one of the straps on my bag had broken, and something about it spoke right to my heart. The broken bag that sat in my hands amidst the pouring rain was the gentle sign of grace-filled conviction I needed within that day.

When I moved to Washington, D.C., I was quickly hit with an onslaught of various emotions including excitement, fear, and hope. The novelty of starting somewhere new offered its own sense of delight and demand, and often times the combination steered me towards striving. I'd grab my metaphorical bag and fill it with all of my *shoulds*: I really *should* work on this; I *should* have had this done by now; I *should* be more like that. This list can and does go on.

In the same way, I've noticed that I often stuff my literal bag in a similar manner, filling its space with a mélange of items I don't need but think I should have: two notebooks, five pens, three books, a charger, my wallet, a snack...or two, the bulletin from church, a pack of gum, loose tissues, and the green rain jacket, just in case. I wish I could tell you this list was an exaggeration, but if anything, it's quite possibly an understatement. And here lies a metaphor for how I often live: filling myself to the brim with the possibility of the days' worth, or my life's worth.

During the Israelite's sojourn through the desert, God provided them with manna: bread through which they were fed. This substance was not void of divine instructions, however. Hungry and financially insecure as they were, God told them to only take enough for the day.

"Then the Lord said to Moses, 'I will rain down bread from heaven for you. The people are to go out each day and gather *enough for that day*. In this way I will test them and see whether they will follow my instructions'." (Exodus 16:4 NIV. Emphasis added)

While the Israelites might have been insecure about God's provision for them, God was not. In light of His sovereign confidence, He asks them to trust His offering and remain hopeful in their promise. I can't help but place myself within this story. Does God not offer me a manna of my own every day? From financial provision to emotional comfort, time and time again He reminds me that He is here, and He is enough. All too often, my attitude and demeanor are eerily like the Israelites. I hoard my resources, my talents, and my gifts as if there won't be enough for tomorrow. As if I don't serve a limitless God. But day after day, God greets me with grace and reminds me that He is, indeed, enough.

Just as the Israelites were challenged to routinely place their trust in God through accepting the allowance He had provided them, the breaking of my shoulder bag felt like a small reminder to do the same. I don't have to stuff my life with a self-fulfillment mentality.

Rather, I can open my metaphorical bag filled with my resources, gifts, hopes and dreams, and empty it day after day, asking God to fill me instead.

Here I will truly see and know that God will always be enough to satisfy.

- *Where in your life are you "overpacking", rather than relying on the faithful provision of God?*
- *How is God calling you to re-adjust?*

Cup 29 | A Table in the Wilderness

"You prepare a table before me in the presence of my enemies. You anoint my head with oil; my cup overflows. Surely your goodness and love will follow me all the days of my life, and I will dwell in the house of the Lord forever."

Psalm 23:5&6 NIV

I have always loved Psalm 23. As a child, it made me feel safe. As a teenager, it made me feel seen. As an adult, it reminds me that I am cared for. This Psalm is not a wishy-washy recital of praise. Rather, I believe it is a deep declaration of the character of God. Our God is a caretaker, provider, protector, and defender. God is a faithful leader and giver of life. With each verse, we are drawn into new depth concerning the intentions of God, and most recently, I have been captivated by verse five – "you prepare a table before me in the presence of my enemies."

In the past, this verse had not taken much root in my heart. Amidst all the other analogies and word pictures, I was quick to read over this sentiment. Recently, however, my friend, Christin, challenged me to pay attention to the ways God had prepared a table for me in the wilderness before and the ways He is doing so in the present. To understand this concept more fully, I did some research.

In ancient Israel, to "prepare a table" was to demonstrate an act of hospitality. The word *prepare* derives from the Hebrew word *arak*, which means to arrange or order. Preparing a table for someone demonstrated a sense of provision and protection within the context of the relationship.

Therefore, God preparing a table for us, inherently implies that we are seen, taken care of, and provided for by God, even in the darkness.

Sounds simple enough, yet so often I fail to grasp its worth. God does not solely wait for the mountaintops to demonstrate His intentional hospitality. Rather, He also uses the wilderness to display the depth of His love. In the valley, we are carried; in the desert, we are led to water; and in the wilderness, we are drawn to eat. God's providence transcends beyond our necessity and enters into His desire to care.

Perhaps our *tables* are found in the various ways we are drawn to witness the presence of God. Laughter. Sunshine. Random acts of grace and kindness. Peace. Protection. Demonstrations of justice here on earth. Maybe these are the ways we are drawn to experience the intentional love of God, even amidst the dark passages of our day.

- *How did God prepare a table in the wilderness for you last week?*
- *How is God doing so today?*

Cup 30 | The Choice

Luke 10:38-42

The story of Martha and Mary (found in Luke chapter 10) has always been one of my favorites. This story invites us to sit within a distinct tension, nestled between the person we may resign to be and the person we desire to become. There is a familiar storyline here; time and time again we are called to see it:

1. Martha was busy and distracted.
2. Mary was focused and attentive.
3. Be like Mary.

I believe this message has its place, but recently a mentor invited me to see things with new perspective, offering that there is more we can glean from the conversation between Martha and Jesus.

"But Martha was distracted by all the preparations that had to be made. She came to him and asked, 'Lord, don't you care that my sister has left me to do the work by myself? Tell her to help me!'" (Luke 10:40 NIV)

At this time in history, it was the job of the women to prepare a meal for the guests. Entertaining Jesus and his crew was no small honor, and if there was nothing to eat at the end of his teaching, all eyes would have been on Martha. In the midst of her frustration, she relays the question on her heart, "Lord, don't you *care?*" With a single request she reminds us of our complex humanity. Martha is not just busy. She is worried. *Lord, do you even care that there is still so much to be done and no one is in my corner to help?* Maybe Martha's response was not so much sass towards Mary, but an inquiry of the intentions of God.

Lord, don't you even care? – Do we not often wonder the same?

And then there's Jesus, who in His infinitely gracious manner, responds not with angered frustration but tenderness and grace.

"Martha, Martha,
        I see you.
You are worried and anxious about many things
        I know there are things to be done. I know that things seem incomplete.
But few things are needed – or indeed, only one. Mary has chosen what is better, and it will not be taken away from her."
        These tasks are not the most important. In fact, Mary has chosen that which is, and the choice is yours as well.

In an instant Christ responds with vision, inviting Martha into a different mindset. He does not diminish what she set out to accomplish; rather He re-introduces her to what will last. And maybe Christ is offering us the same today. While there are many roles and responsibilities, both big and small, that we may face, Christ invites us to sit in His presence *first*, learning to rest at His feet, in order to respond to the tasks at hand. Just like Mary and Martha, the choice is ours today.

· *Where in your life are your questioning, "Lord, do you even care?"*
· *How is God calling you to respond?*

Cup 31 | Carpe Diem

"And if it is evil in your eyes to serve the Lord, choose this day whom you will serve...
But as for me and my house, we will serve the Lord."

Joshua 24:15 ESV

I have always loved the familiar Latin phrase *carpe diem* (seize the day). I've never been one to fully embrace spontaneity as much as I wish, so concepts like this one tend to fuel me with a certain wishful thinking. In all actuality, I'm a planner. Give me a map and I'll follow, but a step by step type of life has never really been my forte. God, however, works much differently, and oftentimes it feels as though He is gently whispering "Just trust me one more time." I believe there is something deeply valuable to be learned here, and maybe phrases like *carpe diem* can lend voice to the beautiful daily rhythms of faith.

In Matthew chapter eight (verses 18-22), a scribe declares to Jesus that he wants to follow him. To my surprise, Jesus responds: "Foxes have holes and birds of the air have nests, but the Son of man has no place to lay his head." Later, a disciple relays that he must first bury his father before journeying with the Lord. Again, I am surprised by Jesus' response: "Follow me, and leave the dead to bury their own dead."

For many years, I was perplexed by this passage. I questioned what burial practices or housing opportunities had to do with following God? I was confused because these requests seemed only natural and worthwhile. The described individuals were not suggesting luxurious desires. Rather, they were offering honest concerns. I have since learned that Jesus' statement was less about physical spaces or customary practices, and more a lesson on values. Jesus was instructing his followers to build their lives on something that would last.

This way of living can be difficult. In a world where we love plans of action and laid-out journeys, dropping everything to live step-by-step is quite scary. Scripture demonstrates, however, that it is always worthwhile. Throughout the Bible, God frequently asks His children to trust in Him above all else, and in doing so, they are invited into a life of freedom. When we focus more on trust than control, we are released from the need to have it all figured out. Instead, we are encouraged to tune our hearts to the melody of God's will. With this type of living, we are always on an adventure.

Maybe concepts like *seize the day*, as they relate to faith, are not as complex or idealistic as we might want to believe. Perhaps sometimes they are as beautiful and simple as waking up and choosing to trust in God all over again.

· *How is God inviting you to trust Him today?*

Cup 32 | A Story to Tell

"Let the redeemed of the Lord tell their story – those he redeemed from the hand of the foe. Let them give thanks to the LORD for his unfailing love and his wonderful deeds for mankind, for he satisfies the thirsty and fills the hungry with good things.

Psalm 107:2,8-9 NIV

One of my favorite narratives in scripture is Jesus' encounter with the Samaritan woman at the well (John 4:1-46). Though society had forced her to the margins, Christ saw her and gave her a voice. What a testament to the gospel: no one is disqualified from being a messenger of its worth. While there is much to glean from this story, I am particularly intrigued by the Samaritan woman's response to her encounter with Christ.

"Just then his disciples returned and were surprised to find him talking with a woman. But no one asked, 'What do you want?' or 'Why are you talking with her?'

Then, leaving her water jar, the woman went back to the town and said to the people, 'Come, see a man who told me everything I ever did. Could this be the Messiah?' They came out of the town and made their way toward him." (John 4: 27-30 NIV)

Notice how Jesus does not rush her into the streets boldly proclaiming: *"This is my daughter. I love her, and you should too."* Rather, instantly compelled to speak of her encounter with the living God, she runs to tell her story, and because of this, an entire community is drawn to seek Christ for themselves.

The Bible is full of stories of people who encountered the Lord and were sent out to share as a result. I believe the same is still true today! As Psalm 107:2 tells us *"Let the redeemed of the Lord tell their story – those he redeemed from the hand of the foe."*

Out for coffee recently with a mentor, I was challenged to consider the divine implications of storytelling. Particularly, their importance in relation to the gospel. If God is, was, and always has been perfect, why does He rely on human words and hands to relay its message? This question both challenged me and ignited my soul with a certain fire. In reflecting on the story of the Samaritan woman, I believe we are given a response. Perhaps Jesus asks us to be His storytellers because He desires for us to be active participants in its continuation.

Wherever God meets us – the kitchen, conference, grocery store, etc. – is fertile ground for a transformative story of hope. Our stories, though different in nature, carry a common theme of redemption. This week, let's trust that our encounters with God can encourage others to seek the same.

- *What is your story?*
- *Who can you share it with this week?*

Cup 33 | Returning to Hope

"Why, my soul, are you downcast? Why so disturbed within me? Put your hope in God, for I will yet praise him, my Savior and my God."

Psalm 42:5 NIV

Towards the end of my semester in Cape Town, I found myself within an intricate blend of emotions. At the time, there was intense tension within the United States that felt palpable, even all the way in South Africa. Personally, I was in the middle of preparing for my last semester of college. *Where would I go next? How would I pay off my student loans? Who had I become during my study abroad experience?* The overthinker in me began to go into overdrive.

On one end, I was excited to return home and finally see my family and friends, but on the other end, I was apprehensive. I knew that life would look different. People were different. I was different. The United States was different. Everything seemed to be in a shifting state.

In the midst of my various emotions, I was often asked a familiar question:

"Natalie, what's next?"

To which I would respond:

"I'll be returning to Hope in the spring."

In all actuality, I meant my college and the people within it, but over time I began to mean the concept as well.

My words became a quiet and personal resolution to actually choose to practice grace, patience, and trust in the midst of a world that was so quickly changing. I realized that I could intentionally choose to recognize the difference, brokenness, and pain, while also acknowledging the light, beauty, and grace that lay within the unknown.

Perhaps we could all use a bit of the same. Life does not always feel hopeful, but luckily, we are not told to find hope in our circumstances. As scripture repeatedly tells us, our hope is only worthwhile when it is placed in something of value.

Though I no longer return to Hope (the institution) with as much frequency, since graduation, hope as a daily practice is something I continue to pursue with confidence. As Psalm 42 states, "Put your hope in *God*, for I will yet praise him, my Savior and my God."

- *Where and how are you finding hope this week?*
- *How are you noticing God in the world around you?*

Cup 34 | Little Miracles

"And whatever you do, whether in word or deed, do it all in the name of the Lord Jesus, giving thanks to God the Father through him."

Colossians 3:17 NIV

One of my favorite books, *Cold Tangerines* by Shauna Niequist, explores the idea of daily celebration in the midst of tumultuous times. It is a declaration of present beauty in the midst of present brokenness, and in a world constantly screaming its faults, I am delighted to remember to give thanks for all that is good.

My favorite chapter in this collection of essays discusses a red tree. Shauna retells a season of her life that was filled with pressing demands. On a random afternoon in the middle of the chaos, she was stopped by a gorgeous fall tree changing colors right across from her home. The tree had gone unnoticed for weeks and in the midst of her hustle, it remained tall, beautiful, and strong. It was this tree, this robust red tree, that stopped her in her tracks, forcing her to realize that her focus had been placed on the wrong things. She saw schedules, events, and to-do lists, yet there were also celebrations, miracles, and God's goodness all around. For me, reading this story became my own red tree – an unsuspecting call to stop and truly observe the life that was going unnoticed before me.

At the time, I was in the middle of my semester in Cape Town; classes had ceased due to campus protests and I was quickly running out of money.

Anxious about the increasing uncertainty of the semester, I began to lose sight of all the miracles that were taking place. The friends I had made, experiences I had embarked upon, the knowledge I'd been privileged to gain; it was all passing me by without much pause for thanksgiving.

At one point, I remarked to one of the other study-abroad students that things had begun to feel rather normal for me. I had lost the thrill of being abroad. He responded with a bit of shock.

"Really!? How can you look at Table Mountain and not be amazed?"

Suddenly I was offered another *red tree*. In the midst of worry, uncertainty, and busyness, there was striking beauty all around me and I needed to pay more attention.

There's a lot to be anxious about if we want to be, but I believe there are also hundreds of blessings that far too often go unnoticed. In the middle of the chaos, it is easy to lose sight of grace – a precious gift that seems to whisper, *things don't always have to be as you thought they'd be, but they can still be good.*

In every broken thing there lies the potential for beauty. We cannot live with our eyes closed, or more times than not we'll miss the daily blessings of being alive. I don't want to face my day, or life for that matter, oblivious to the beauty of God's present grace. I want to see, acknowledge, and cherish my little miracles. I hope yours are more apparent this week as well.

- *What blessings went unnoticed in your life last week?*
- *How can you be sure to live with eyes wide open this week?*

Cup 35 | The Middle

"And without faith it is impossible to please him, for whoever would draw near to God must believe that he exists and that he rewards those who seek him.

Hebrews 11:6 ESV

It's a little before 5 p.m. I'm at my local Panera, iced coffee in hand, contemplating how I will finish this book. As of now, there are about 20 reflections left to be edited. I am tired and a bit anxious, but hopeful nonetheless. Truthfully, on more than one occasion the past few weeks, I have wanted to give up. This whole book idea feels quite scary when I truly acknowledge what I am doing, and yet – a still small voice tells me, "Keep going." So here we are.

Writing has become both a practice and deep-seated prayer for me. It is a physical demonstration of patience and trust, two reminders I often need. At the beginning of things, I am excited – awakened to the multitude of thoughts in my head. I take a deep breath as I begin to place the words onto the page, but then something stops me – I get tired, stuck or bored, and I want to give up or try something new. Most times, these emotions are simply masking deeper insecurities. I fear my words are not good enough. I question if my thoughts are worth sharing. And in doing so, I minimize the importance of the process.

One thing writing this book has taught me is that writing – just like life – requires a deep, wholehearted commitment to the process. Writing and creating, for that matter, necessitate trust that the monotonous details are necessary and worthwhile, for without them we get no end result. And what I keep finding, much to my dismay, is that so much of life's necessary growth components lie within the middle.

I hate the middle; it's exactly where I want to give up. In the middle I am tempted to forgo what I've begun because – well there's less to lose. But what I am learning is that it is exactly within the middle where we are also given the opportunity to practice courage. In the middle we are given chances to debunk our fears of inadequacy and desire for perfection. In the space between our starts and stops, we can be taught grace, persistence, and valor. As we are forced to choose grit over fear and stamina over defeat, we are reminded that we are stronger than we think.

Hebrews 11:1 tells us, *"Now faith is being sure of what we hope for and certain of what we do not see."* This chapter then goes on to list several examples of people who had to demonstrate wholehearted faith in order to fulfill God's purpose for their life. Noah did not build the ark once the rain began, just as Abraham waited not for ultimate clarity to sojourn. With each step, these Biblical pillars of faith demonstrated deeper acts of hope. And I am learning that hope rests in incompletion, for it calls us to respond well without the end in sight. With each story of true faith in the Bible, we are shown an ending full of worthwhile rewards. I believe this is the very thing that can propel us in the middle. Though we work in hopes of what *could be* and not necessarily what *is*, our obedience to God lends voice to a result that is always worth the wait.

While the middle offers a great deal of imperfection: words left unsaid, inconsistencies unresolved, and conclusions yet to be drawn, it also offers a great deal of hope. Perhaps the middle is a lot more of a sacred space than I ever realized; I believe this to be true even with this book.

I must keep writing because I believe I have something to say. I must keep praying because I believe God hears me. I must keep dreaming because I believe there is work to be done. I pray you do too.

- *Where do you currently find yourself in the middle?*
- *What scripture do you need to cling to, to keep moving forward?*

Cup 36 | Dancing in the Rain

"I know what it is to be in need, and I know what it is to have plenty. I have learned the secret of being content in any and every situation, whether well fed or hungry, whether living in plenty or in want. I can do all this through him who gives me strength."

Philippians 4:12&13 NIV

As I write these words, it's raining outside, a slow and still type of rain. Everyone around me is asleep and I should be too, but all I can seem to do is observe the downpour outdoors.

I've been in a spot this season of constantly feeling overwhelmed – physically, emotionally, and spiritually. I'm not good at letting things be when they're unexpected or the conclusion is not in sight. See, I've never been the girl to dance in the rain. In fact, I've always done the opposite. I'm the person who runs to the nearest place of shelter, whether that be inside the house, a car, or even under an umbrella. Unexpected rain has this way of stopping us in our tracks, if even only to acknowledge its presence. It is in this space that we are given options: we can run and hide, waiting for the sun to come out, or we can stop and dance.

I've always been intrigued by those that take the time to enjoy the beautiful simplicity of dancing in the rain. It's as if they've learned this secret of being content in the midst of life's obstacles. I think dancing in the rain is a beautiful picture of receiving the moment for what it is and not what we wish it to be. In doing so, we are able to experience the fullness of what the day has to offer – the beauty, pain, and even monotony.

In Philippians chapter four, Paul offers us a model of contentment, as he states, *"I know what it is to be in need, and I know what it is to have plenty. I have learned the secret of being content in any and every situation, whether well fed or hungry, whether living in plenty or in want. I can do all this through him who gives me strength."*

At the time of this decree, Paul was not living the good life. He was actually in prison exemplifying the essence of this statement. In everything, we can find a reason to give thanks.

There are mornings when the toast burns and the bills are more than expected. There are evenings that end too late and days that start too early. There are seasons when life just doesn't make sense. But what do we do with these moments? Do we run, hide and wait for better days, do we make to-do lists on how to fix it? Or do we allow ourselves the opportunity to experience the rain?

I believe dancing in the rain invites us to stop and feel, reminding us that life is so much bigger than the complexity of our problems or unexpected circumstances. Here we are given a chance to feel something, not in spite of the rain, but because of it.

As I mentioned, I've never been one for dancing in the rain. In fact, I've always done the opposite, but today, I choose to seek my own dancing in the rain moments. I hope you do the same.

- *Where are you finding God in the rain?*
- *How can you lean into the beauty of life's unexpected moments this week?*

Cup 37 | An Open Letter to September

"Look at the birds of the air; they do not sow or reap or store away in barns, and yet your heavenly Father feeds them. Are you not much more valuable than they?"

Matthew 6:26 NIV

Dear September,

Welcome back – although, in all honesty, I wasn't exactly looking forward to your presence. It's not that I don't love your colors, or the last late-night bonfires you foster, or even the way you infuse pumpkin spice into everything; rather I am resistant to the way you epitomize change.

You must be well-acquainted with change. Each year you watch school kids exchange sand buckets for backpacks. You witness parents whisper tearful goodbyes into the ears of college freshmen. You watch as backyard decor slowly makes its way into the garage. And you hold all these things in your hand – but me? Every year I know you are coming, yet every year I find myself surprised by how different life looks when you are around. Within your 30-day time slot, you loudly announce to the world: *It's time for something new!* You have this way of embodying the transition that occurs as life shifts from one end of the spectrum to another, and this is hard. It is challenging to sit in the middle of life's shifting and be content.

I've always wanted to be the girl that remembered the *lilies* – the one who took that verse on worry and contentment in Matthew 6 seriously. If I'm honest, however, sometimes the lilies are the last thing I want to think about in the midst of everything looking, sounding, and feeling different.

But September, in the midst of your changing colors and unpredictable weather, you remind me of a truth I so often forget. A truth that whispers *we are all called to show up and ask for directions.* I guess we're not always invited to see the inner workings behind the process of change. Sometimes we must simply observe their effects. You remind me that while it is hard to see how change is actually *changing* the world around us, it is here that true trust comes into play. Trust that there is beauty and good on the other side, trust that seasons truly do happen for a reason, and trust that things don't always have to go according to our plan to be good.

September, you remind me to trust the necessity and process of change, because maybe if life always looked the way it does in June and the sun always shone the way it does in July, I'd get a bit comfortable, forgetting to look around and observe the mystery of life unfolding all around me. Perhaps when I begin to feel off balance, it is then that I am forced to see the greater hand at work in the changes around me.

So, September, I'll try not to dread the changes you bring this year or wish away your timing. As the world continues to embrace the unique differences you carry versus the ones that came from the months before, I'll try to embrace them as well.

- *I encourage you to take a solo walk this week and appreciate the changing seasons at hand. What sticks out to you?*

Cup 38 | Here

"Then he said to him, 'Follow me!'"

John 21:15-19 NIV

W ho do you turn to when you're disappointed? Where do you go when life no longer looks like it used to? I believe these are worthwhile questions, for at some point or another, we have all experienced our fair share of let-downs. How could life change, however, if we allowed these back-to-reality moments to make us stronger? Who could we become, if we allowed the everyday experiences of our lives to become the best parts of our lives?

In his critically acclaimed book, *My Utmost for His Highest*, Oswald Chambers writes about the danger of solely seeking mountaintop experiences. I find his words to be extremely encouraging, especially as they relate to our daily walk of following the Lord. This week may his words serve as a reminder to us all, to find God in the complexity of the ordinary.

The Sphere of Exaltation by Oswald Chambers

"We are not built for the mountains and the dawns and aesthetic affinities, those are for moments of inspiration, that is all. We are built for the valley, for the ordinary stuff we are in, and that is where we have to prove our mettle. Spiritual selfishness always wants repeated moments on the mount. We feel we could talk like angels and live like angels, if only we could stay on the mount. The times of exaltation are exceptional, they have their meaning in our life with God, but we must beware lest our spiritual selfishness wants to make them the only time.

We are apt to think that everything that happens is to be turned into useful teaching, it is to be turned into something better than teaching, viz., into character. The mount is not meant to teach us anything, it is meant to make us something. There is a great snare in asking — "What is the use of it?" In spiritual matters we can never calculate on that line. The moments on the mountain tops are rare moments, and they are meant for something in God's purpose."

· *What sticks out to you from this quote?*
· *How is God calling you to be present in your spiritual walk this week?*

Cup 39 | A Call Amidst the Chaos

"But remember the Lord your God, for it is he who gives you the ability to produce wealth, and so confirms his covenant, which he swore to your ancestors, as it is today."

Deuteronomy 8:18 NIV

During my post-graduate year in D.C., I couldn't help but notice a glaring concern, not too dissimilar from that of the rest of the world. Washington, D.C. is noticeably marked by its contradictions. In the shadows of ivory towers lie the vulnerable and unprotected. On the fringes of power remain the voiceless. *The first shall be last and the last shall be first* – feels a lot more like wishful thinking than Biblical mandate. In the heart of this city there is both a yearning for change and a deep fear it will never come. I think this is often the paradox of being human, yet maybe it is also the tension of hope.

Occasionally, I found it difficult to choose hope while I was there. I questioned, *how can I choose hope when so many live below the poverty line and my timeline continues to fill with stories of tragedy?* Amid all that was broken, I was forced to face the size of my incapable hands. I did not have the means or strength to bring about the hope I desired.

So, *to be or not to be?* This question danced through my mind on many given days as I confronted all that was beautiful and broken before me. In a world so noticeably stained by its painful disposition, how do we find hope?

In Deuteronomy 8, the Israelites are given a call to remember. *Do not forget,* the Lord repeats. *Do not forget the times I have carried you. Do not forget my provision. Do not forget my protection. Do not forget Me.* I can't help but think that the same is asked of us today. When we process this world through the lens of our circumstances and not the character of God, we are quick to forget His faithfulness. When pride and privilege infiltrate our sense of self sufficiency, the walls of our limitations are quickly exposed.

Grace, however, meets us as we hit these walls, bringing us to a place of complete dependence on Christ. I find this to be simultaneously freeing and frightening. Frightening because of the unknown, yet freeing because God knows the unknown. It is within this tension that we are offered hope. This hope is something much bigger than words on a page; rather it is a force requiring action, courage, and trust even within external uncertainty. Sometimes it takes everything we have to choose faith over fear, trust over doubt, hope over despondency, but it is here that our hope is sustained.

How can we not be hopeful when we've chosen to believe in the power of Christ's redemption? How can we not be hopeful when we've *experienced* the power of Christ's redemption? This world is unavoidably messy, chaotic and broken, *and* Christ is making all things new. Hope is this promise amidst the tension. Hope is trust in this promise *despite* the tension.

Yes, Washington, D.C. is, indeed, a city noticeably marked by its contradictions. Every day, while there, I was forced to confront how small my hands truly were, yet even so, every day this city gave me another reason to put my hope in something much bigger than myself. For this, I am grateful.

- *How is God calling you to respond to the circumstances around you?*
- *Where do you see grace in the midst of chaos?*

Part IV.

Cup 40 | A New Song

Psalm 96

D uring my time in Cape Town, I made a friend named Collins, who was equally a poet and intellect at heart. Collins always left me with something new and striking to think about after each of our interactions. One afternoon, we discussed our dreams and where we wanted to be in the world in a few years' time. The dreams we had for ourselves were beautiful and scary in their own right, and when I confessed my timidity towards the enormity of my own life goals, he shared a story of home.

When Collins was younger, and his mother bought him new clothes, she'd always buy jackets a size or two too big. This, of course, was intentional, for she knew that with just the right amount of time and space he'd grow into the items at hand. He then went on to tell me how he had found a life metaphor within this concept: Sometimes life and the contexts we find ourselves in seem far too big for our own capabilities, but it is here that we are invited to grow.

I left our conversation that sunny afternoon, inspired, hopeful, but more than anything, intrigued. If God laid out a similar concept in my own life, then maybe the things I deem too big do not have to scare me after all.

Psalm 96 instructs us to sing to the Lord a new song, and when I think about it, this feels a lot like putting on a new jacket, maybe even an oversized one. To try on something new implies replacing something old and here we are given the freedom to grow. Perhaps

---

God challenges us to begin again, declaring the faithfulness of His cause and the lives we have been given as a result. Like sweaters that have become far too small, we too grow out of familiar codes of conduct. To refrain from growing stagnant, complacent, or even stifled, we are placed in situations that challenge and invite us to make a change.

I will admit, when I truly make time and space to listen to the voice of God, I am sometimes terrified by where I feel His leading. God's plans for me are always far bigger than my own, and it is so good, and oftentimes so very scary. With this said, what Collins taught me through his recollective story of life, growth, and motherhood is that parents invest in the process. They expect experiential growth and prepare us for the result. So maybe God, too, places us in circumstances and situations beyond our capabilities, not because He wants us to drown within them, but rather because He knows that with time, grace, and faith, we, too, will grow.

- *What in your life currently feels like an oversized jacket?*
- *How is God calling you to grow?*

Cup 41 | It is I

*"When he was at the table with them, he took bread, gave thanks, broke
it and began to give it to them. Then their eyes were opened and they recognized
him, and he disappeared from their sight.*

Luke 24:30&31 NIV

A few weeks ago, a friend relayed to me how complicated her life had become. The circumstances around her were growing too much to bear, and she questioned: "Where is God in all of this?"

The question lingered in the air for a few moments, as I was reminded of the times I've questioned the same. Later that evening, I remembered a similar scenario experienced by the disciples in Luke 24. Jesus was recently crucified, and the disciples were hurting. As they were journeying on the road to Emmaus, Jesus appeared to them but kept his identity hidden, so they could not recognize him.
As they walked together, the disciples explained their anguish, stating:

"'Are you the only visitor to Jerusalem who does not know the things that have happened there in these days?' And he said to them, 'What things?' And they said to him, 'Concerning Jesus of Nazareth, a man who was a prophet mighty in deed and word before God and all the people, and how our chief priests and rulers delivered him up to be condemned to death, and crucified him. But we had hoped that he was the one to redeem Israel.'" (Luke 24:19-21)

Here the disciples described their frustration and loss of hope. Though Jesus had told them repeatedly of the events that would come to pass while he was on earth, the events they experienced led them to fear. It's easy to look at the disciples with a bit of confusion. They were foretold what would come to pass by Jesus, himself. How could they forget? When we stop and contemplate their situation in relation to our own, we might find that we easily exemplify the same. In our moments of uncertainty and confusion, it is easy to run to doubt, forgetting the hope God has given us time after time throughout His word.

What I love most about this story is that Jesus does not dismiss the disciples due to their unbelief. Instead, he takes time to relay the prophecies. Shortly thereafter, captivated by his presence, without fully knowing they are entertaining the risen Lord, the disciples invite Jesus to stay for dinner.

"So he went in to stay with them. When he was at table with them, he took the bread and blessed and broke it and gave it to them. And their eyes were opened, and they recognized him. And he vanished from their sight. They said to each other, 'Did not our hearts burn within us while he talked to us on the road, while he opened to us the Scriptures?'" (Luke 24:29-32)

Through the breaking of bread and the participation of community, Christ re-identifies himself. Suddenly, as they begin to eat, the disciples are more apt to recognize their risen Lord. I believe we are reminded through this story that God does not always appear in the ways we expect. His arrival is not usually with triumphant symbols and flashy words; occasionally, and maybe even most times, it is through the slow, still, rhythmic process of being with the Lord. Here, we are reminded that He has been with us all along.

- *How did God meet you in the unexpected last week?*
- *How might God be concealed within the unexpected today?*

Cup 42 | Walking on Broken Glass

"I lift up my eyes to the hills. From where does my help come? My help comes from the Lord, who made heaven and earth."

Psalm 121:1&2 NIV

After returning home from my time in D.C., many people asked me about my overall experience. Oddly, I often didn't know what to say. While the time I had spent was still relatively fresh, the series of events that occurred while there felt rather hazy. Washington, D.C. was such a strange place to be at that time. The country was so divided, divisive, and dysfunctional. I entered D.C. on the tail of the Charlottesville protest and in just a short amount of time after, Hurricane Maria, #Metoo, and the Vegas shooting occurred. Sadly, this is only the short list. With great haste, the world began to resemble that of a shattered snow globe. I could not move without stepping on top of yet another sharp edge, and as I sat in the nation's capital – the place supposedly filled with so much power and momentum for change – I felt helpless and unable to move forward.

Shortly before leaving for D.C., my grandmother encouraged me to recite Psalm 121 every morning: *I will lift my eyes to the hills. From where does my help come? My help comes from the Lord.*

I have since learned that this is a Song of Ascent, intended to serve as a cry of confidence for those making the pilgrimage to Jerusalem. Back then, this voyage – in its completion, served as metaphor for the journey of life, a picturesque reminder that in God we do not have to be afraid. Though we walk through dark and desperate times, we have a caretaker to whom we can run.

Within Psalm 121 lies a call to look up in order to look down. In looking to the hill, we are given vertical perspective in light of horizontal vision, and this makes all the difference. Suddenly we are able to see beyond what is right before us, and as a result, we are able to face the journey with greater expectation. Though the shards of life are sharp and heavy, they do not present themselves without the hope of redemption.

What I discovered in Washington, D.C. is that when my grandmother encouraged me to recite this Psalm each morning, she gave me something much greater than a suggested daily rhythm. Rather, she offered me a method to face the madness. When we look to God and not our own means of survival, we are always reminded that we do not face the brokenness alone.

·   *How is God showing you beauty in the midst of brokenness this week?*
·   *How is God calling you to look toward redemption?*

Cup 43 | The Invisible Line

"Now faith is the assurance of things hoped for, the conviction of things not seen..."

Hebrews 11:1 ESV

I remember the sudden shock I felt the second my friend, Camryn, shut down her laptop and exclaimed,

"That's it! I am officially done with my undergraduate career."

The moment itself was no surprise. We were five days away from graduation, and yet the finality of our college career grabbed me in that moment with visceral force. The days, weeks, and months prior to my graduation felt like living in an unpredictable universe. In some sense, most seniors appeared to be chickens with their heads cut off – in motion, yet entirely unaware of what came next. The distance to the finish line was not for the unprepared.

I read a blog post at the time about choosing faith over fear, courage over despair. The writer symbolized the space between where we are and where we are going as an invisible line. At the time of reading this post, my invisible lines felt quite visible, so this analogy sat with me deeply.

So much of this life seems to resemble an invisible line. We are always in front of another unknown or *could be*. All too often I am desperate to know what lies on the other side. *Who will I meet? What will happen as a result? Who will I become in the process?* The words in that post, however, challenged me to think differently. The future should not sit on the back of my uncertainty; rather, it should rest in the arms of my faith. As Hebrews 11 instructs us, faith is a certain *knowing*, even despite the unknown. When I choose to demonstrate confidence in the sovereignty and goodness of God rather than fear my own capabilities and limitations, I lean into a strength and power much greater than my own. I believe this mentality offers us an invitation towards a different kind of life, one that is exceptionally more expectant, celebratory, and hopeful.

With every beginning, there lies an invisible line – the possibility of what's next and the unknown of what will be. This week, in the midst of my invisible lines, I plan to demonstrate more faith. I hope you do too.

- *What invisible lines stand before you this week?*
- *What are 3 ways you can intentionally demonstrate more faith?*

Cup 44 | A Beautiful Mess

"He has told you, O man, what is good; and what does the Lord require of you
but to do justice, and to love kindness, and to walk humbly with your God?"

Micah 6:8 ESV

M y friend Katlyn is brilliant. She is equal parts spontaneity and discipline – a combination, I've found, that is quite rare. My junior year of college, we were housemates, living and learning in an intentional community known as the Emmaus Scholars. The Emmaus Scholars was a program created to foster a deeper Biblical understanding of the Church's call and response to social justice issues. For a year, we pored over literature, experiences, and conversations centered on what was broken and how Christ was calling us to participate in His redemption. This was hard, scary, and undoubtedly necessary.

With each passing day, I was drawn towards a world that was irrevocably broken and a Savior who was making all things new. The tension was palpable. It still is. The thing about pain, however, if I can quote a line from *The Fault in Our Stars*, is that "it demands to be felt." And that it was. On a personal level, I began to feel more deeply the weight of structural brokenness concerning race in America. But more than that, I began to see the ways my eyes had been blinded for so long from other issues that deeply affected those around me. These issues were not just the problems of others – they are issues for the Church.

The daily call to notice and respond grew overwhelming at times, and this made raw and honest conversations all the more necessary. Over the course of the year, I found Katlyn to be a confidant of sorts, always holding my questions in tension with both faith and intellect. We would spend hours discussing the world, its issues, and its Hope, and then: when it was finally way past our bedtimes – we'd pray.

One evening, Katlyn closed her prayer with a line I'll never forget. I'd like to share it with you too:

"And, Lord, although this life is messy, help us to remember that it is also beautiful."

At a time when the mess felt much more consuming than the beauty, these words stopped me in my tracks and gave me hope. A clear reminder of the *both/and* of a life of faith. Though there is evident brokenness, there is also present redemption. A grace that supersedes all. This is something worth noticing. This is something for which I ought to give more thanks. This week, may we remember that there is beauty despite the mess and give thanks for a God who meets us within both.

- *What in your life is messy at the moment?*
- *How can you meet God there this week?*

Cup 45 | Consider the Cherry Blossoms

"Consider the lilies how they grow, they do not labor or spin. Yet I tell you, not even Solomon in all his splendor was dressed like one of these. If that is how God clothes the grass of the field, which is here today, and tomorrow is thrown into the fire, how much more will he clothe you."

Luke 12:27&28 NIV

If all goes well and winter is gracious in Washington, D.C., the cherry blossom trees begin to bloom in early April. They are simply majestic, offering the city a gentle glow with their soft shades of pink and white. During my time there, these beautiful buds reminded me a lot of Jesus' command in Luke 12: *Consider the lilies how they grow, they do not labor or spin. Yet I tell you, not even Solomon in all his splendor was dressed like one of these.*

Worry is all too easy a default. It can quickly become the placeholder between faith and fear. In a time so full of present-day mishaps and blatant evil, worry seems like a plausible option. *If we only find the correct solution, then things will go according to plan. If we just set the right intentions and follow through, then we can be at ease.* Occasionally, this is true. We need discipline and direction to live life well, but when we make Control our god, as it is all too easy to do, we quickly lose sight of that which is truly important. We leave little room for grace. And grace is the thing that keeps us steady as it meets us amid our worries, troubles, and fears. Grace reminds us that God is so much more powerful than the ideas, notions, and solutions we create for ourselves. This idea is demonstrated in Matthew 14.

"Shortly before dawn Jesus went out to them, walking on the lake. When the disciples saw him walking on the lake, they were terrified.

'It's a ghost,' they said, and cried out in fear.
But Jesus immediately said to them: 'Take courage! It is I. Don't be afraid.'
      'Lord, if it's you,' Peter replied, 'tell me to come to you on the water.'

      'Come,' he said.

Then Peter got down out of the boat, walked on the water and came toward Jesus. But when he saw the wind, he was afraid and, beginning to sink, cried out,

      'Lord, save me!'

Immediately Jesus reached out his hand and caught him.
'You of little faith,' he said, 'why did you doubt?' And when they climbed into the boat, the wind died down. Then those who were in the boat worshiped him, saying, 'Truly you are the Son of God.'"
(Matthew 14:25-32 NIV)

While I admire the courageous faith of Peter and the love of God extended with a gentle hand, I often forget to consider the aftermath. Could it be that Peter returned to the boat sopping wet and a bit shaken? Before his friends, fellow disciples, and Jesus Christ, Peter tried, failed, and tried again. As he dried his eyes, shook his hair, and took a seat, maybe he felt embarrassed...maybe he felt hope?

In Peter's act of faith, he was drawn to consider his limitations, and in reaching them he was afforded a grace beyond the shore. I don't know what Peter thought when he returned to the boat, but I do know he returned with a story. Peter returned with a deep understanding of Christ's ability to walk on water. In addition, he returned with the experiential realization that when he kept his eyes on Jesus, he could walk on water too. Maybe when we take the time to consider the ways God has shown up in our own lives, we find that we have been afforded the same.

In taking time to notice the splendor of something as seemingly small as cherry blossom trees in D.C, I am reminded to let go and let God. And when I do, I always find that He is more powerful, wonderful, and intentional than I originally believed.

· *How is God calling you to pay attention this week?*

Cup 46 | There is a Time

"I have seen the burden God has laid on the human race. He has made everything beautiful in its time. He has also set eternity in the human heart; yet no one can fathom what God has done from beginning to end."

Ecclesiastes 3:10-11 NIV

A few months ago, my place of work held a staff retreat. To open our time together, one of the staff members shared a short devotional on Ecclesiastes 3: *A Time for Everything.* Through personal reflection and Biblical analysis, she depicted the ways that community and faith are essential components of our various seasons. To close her message, she passed out slips of paper containing Ecclesiastes 3:1-8 to each person in the room, asking us to circle what time felt most applicable to our present circumstances. After recollecting these sheets, she began to read aloud what had been circled.

A time to mourn, read one.
A time to dance, read another.
A time to heal... and the list continued.

It was breathtaking. In a room filled with nearly 50 people, there was a vast array of present circumstances. In this moment, the distinction between our various seasons felt extremely raw, real, and hopeful. *There is a time for everything.*

I have since come to love Ecclesiastes 3, for it reminds me that there is room for the unavoidable nuance of this life. Though I may mourn, I will not always be in mourning. Though I may plant, I will not always be waiting for harvest. And in a world where the news is increasingly heartbreaking, and our personal lives never seem to slow down, this feels like a necessary reminder. I can cry while you laugh. You can dance while I mourn, and the two do not have to be mutually exclusive; in fact, they can inform each other. In watching your hope, I, too, can be reminded of my own. In witnessing your tears, I, too, can be invited to feel again.

What I've learned with time is that Ecclesiastes 3 is not solely a declaration of the various seasons we will encounter in life. Rather, it is a communal decree to trust the faithfulness of God in every situation. Though our seasons may vary, our hope in Christ remains the same, and this makes every season something to notice and celebrate.

- *What season are you in?*
- *How is God calling you to pay attention to the season of someone around you?*

Cup 47 | Six Goldfish

"The Lord your God is with you, the Mighty Warrior who saves. He will take great delight in you; in his love he will no longer rebuke you, but will rejoice over you with singing."

Zephaniah 3:17 NIV

This is a story of unconventional hope manifested through spontaneous kindness. I believe God has a sense of humor, and I also believe it takes a little patience and determination to find it. This is just one of the ways I've noticed how.

Towards the end of the first semester, my junior year of college, I started to wish for a pet goldfish. It was a small and insignificant desire, but one that was present nonetheless. Not committed enough to purchase one on my own, I remained content to go without. God, however, had other plans. Shortly before heading home for Christmas vacation, I stopped by my friend Morgan's house to pick up a package. Upon my arrival, I noticed six small goldfish in jars on the table – Henry, Velvet, Gouda, Spoon, Fed-Ex, and Tx., were their names – small fish she had received from two parents who were not yet ready to teach their children about death. She kindly offered them to me and my housemates, and in that moment my heart began to stir, for I knew this was more than mere happenstance. This was divine provision manifested in an incredibly whimsical way.

It's a random story but isn't this just how God works sometimes – in grand moments like dreams and visions, yet also small moments like goldfish in mason jars. In these moments I am reminded of a God who laughs and delights in His children.

Zephaniah 3:17 reminds us that we serve a God who loves deeply, and this love transcends beyond provision or protection and enters into deep-seated care. God loves to the point of delight, and with six small goldfish in the middle of December, I was drawn to see as much.

With six small goldfish, I was reminded that God is never too busy for the small desires of our hearts. His love always supersedes our understanding, and what a gift this continues to be.

· *How has the whimsical love of God manifested itself in your life this week?*

Cup 48 | Songs of Hope

"Oh sing to the Lord a new song; sing to the Lord, all the earth!"

Psalm 96:1 ESV

During a challenging season, *King of my Heart* by Bethel Worship quickly became my anthem of hope. On days when I was tired, frustrated, and emotionally drained I'd turn up my speakers and sing the words:

> *You are good-good-ohhh*
> *You are good-good-ohhh.*

Though I didn't realize it at the time, this practice became revolutionary for me. When my circumstances grew to be more than I could bear, I'd turn on this song, forcing my heart to sing a promise my mind had trouble owning.

> *You (God) are good-good-ohhh*

Singing seems inconsequential at best and silly at worst when we are in the midst of a storm. As the waves of life tumble into our safe havens, choosing to break out into song appears foolish. The Bible, however, is full of accounts of people singing in the midst of dire circumstances.

When Paul and Silas were arrested because of their witness for Christ, and after they were sorely beaten, they gathered together in their jail cell and sang worship to God. When Mary was given unexpected and quite startling news, she ran to Elizabeth with a song in her heart. And David...well this guy always seems to be singing, when life is good and when it isn't.

Fifty-Two Cups of Coffee

For years, I have looked at these stories with a certain admiration. I still do, but when challenges in my personal life continued to arise, I couldn't help wonder, *where did their song of hope come from and why?* In the midst of injustice, fear, and uncertainty, how did these people willfully choose to have a song?

While I was a student at Hope College, I had the privilege of attending a sermon given by Reverend Gabriel Salguero on the topic of courage. Towards the end of his message, he described an experience he had the previous year where he and a group of 70 other pastors were arrested during an act of civil disobedience. From the paddy wagon to the holding cell, they collectively sang:

"Our God is an awesome God He reigns from Heaven above with wisdom, power, and love our God is an awesome God."

Multiple times, apprehension and question were directed towards this group for their song, and at one point, one of the pastors – a 68-year-old man – responded:

"We don't sing because we feel like it. We sing because it brings hope into the room. When we sing, it's telling our circumstance, our calling is greater than our reality."

With this message, I was reminded that our reason to sing is birthed from a greater hope within us. Though our circumstances remain full of questions, uncertainty, and even doubt, we can proclaim a confidence bigger than our fears. The unknown, while challenging and scary, is not void of hope, and for this very reason, I believe we can all find a reason to sing.

- *What song of hope can you cling to this week?*
- *Who in your life do you need to share this song with?*

.

Cup 49 | Water from a Rock

"From the end of the earth I will cry to You, When my heart is overwhelmed; Lead me to the rock that is higher than I."

Psalm 61:2 NKJV

I love blogs. They are my most preferred pastime. One of my favorites is a self-titled website curated by writer and business mogul, Zim Ugochukwu. Recently, she shared a reflection on finding God and purpose even in the desert. While depicting the distinct challenge of our *dry* seasons, she writes:

> *"God often brings us into desert seasons not to harm us, but to prepare us. He will reposition or remove the things that we turn to fill ourselves up. And He'll use that season, while painful, to break, assemble & strengthen us. It's His divine preparation."*

This quote has since challenged me to pay greater attention to the ways God is using the non-desirable circumstances in my life to draw me closer to Him. In Exodus chapter 17, the Israelites – weary from their journey – cry out to Moses for water. The Lord responds by providing rejuvenation through an unconventional source: the crevice of a rock.

> *"But the people were thirsty for water there, and they grumbled against Moses. They said, 'Why did you bring us up out of Egypt to make us and our children and livestock die of thirst?'*
>
> *Then Moses cried out to the Lord, 'What am I to do with these people? They are almost ready to stone me.'*
>
> *The Lord answered Moses, 'Go out in front of the people. Take with you some of the elders of Israel and take in your hand the staff with which you struck the Nile, and go. I will stand there before you by the rock at*

Horeb. Strike the rock, and water will come out of it for the people to drink'. So Moses did this in the sight of the elders of Israel." (Exodus 17:3-6)

We often joke about being caught between a rock and a hard place, but could it be that in these very spaces living water abounds? In the tension of desperation, God offers new life through unique circumstances, and when I look carefully, I find that the Gospel displays this same concept repeatedly. God is continuously using tense and challenging circumstances to demonstrate His authority and love. I must believe the same is no less true today.

Though tiresome, perhaps our desert seasons serve as ideal circumstances to remind us of the intricate power of God. When we pause, weary from a thirst we can't quench on our own, we just might find that God meets us in the most extraordinary and unconventional ways. The spaces we have deemed too dry can ultimately become the rock through which He offers new life. This is the thing that fascinates me most about the desert and our desert seasons. I am learning that they do not necessarily represent the absence of life, but rather serve as a specific space for us to be surprised by where we find it.

· *Where is God offering you new life within the desert today?*

Cup 50 | On Faith

"As Jesus was walking beside the Sea of Galilee, he saw two brothers, Simon called Peter and his brother Andrew. They were casting a net into the lake, for they were fishermen.

'Come, follow me,' Jesus said, 'and I will send you out to fish for people.' **At once they left their nets and followed him.**

Going on from there, he saw two other brothers, James son of Zebedee and his brother John. They were in a boat with their father Zebedee, preparing their nets. Jesus called them, **and immediately they left the boat and their father and followed him."**

Matthew 4:18-21 NIV (emphasis added)

...

This story strikes a chord in me – one I find to be both hopeful and slightly perplexing. In each scenario, the disciples took a risk that required a profound release of control in exchange for trust and dependence on God. While there is so much about this passage that inspires me, I am simultaneously left with many questions. For instance,

> *Who would fill the work roles they had so quickly abandoned?*
> *What became of their father?*
> *What exactly happened to the nets or the fish they were trying to catch?*

In this story, Christ's call was not simply to believe but to act on the belief, and this is where I see faith. In releasing their nets, Peter and

Andrew let go of more than material; they simultaneously released a way of living.

"**Come, follow me,**" Jesus said.

I think the same is asked of us today.

I believe faith is the distance between where we are and where we are called to be. It is the small steps of conviction that in turn move the mountains of change. It is easy to forget this within the process, which is to say, faith can be difficult. It is an unseen inner substance requiring outward participation, but the risk (even in all its complexity) is worth it.

So, what are our nets? What are our areas of self-sufficiency and what would it take for us to drop them all? As we drop our nets of desired control, we are invited to see they were never ours to carry. As we hope in something greater, truer, and exponentially better than what we could create for ourselves, we are drawn to see our bar was set too low.

· *What would it look like to drop your net today?*

Cup 51 | A Moment like This

"For if you keep silent at this time, relief and deliverance will rise for the Jews from another place, but you and your father's house will perish. And who knows whether you have not come to the kingdom for such a time as this?"

Esther 4:14 ESV

Towards the middle of my senior year of college, I was asked to share my story at an upcoming chapel. This was an opportunity to demonstrate the essence of Psalm 107:2 — *Let the redeemed of the Lord say so*. I was both honored and overwhelmed.

In the weeks leading up to my speech date, I felt a gentle internal nudge to speak honestly about my experience as a black student at a predominantly white institution, and the challenges and greater hope I had experienced along the way. I was terrified: scared that I would offend some, misrepresent others, and leave little to no lasting impact. I spent a lot of time during those weeks thinking, praying, and quite honestly crying. The opportunity at hand had exposed a personal wound that had gone unaddressed for far too long. Deep down I believed my story was not worth sharing.

In the book of Esther, I find a similar tension. Though our experiences, circumstances, and qualifications are vastly different, within the chapters of both of our stories lies an underlying call for spiritual boldness. I believe the same is true for us all. In Esther's story, we are quickly met with conflict. From the first chapter and onward, we are invited to witness power abuse, radical resistance, and exile. At the time, Jews were still under an oppressive regime given their status as minorities in Persia, which included Esther. Even with all of this going against her, she is elevated to a position of power.

Later on, Mordecai calls Esther to speak on behalf of the Jewish people, and at first, she is apprehensive. If anyone had a reason to be silent, it was Esther. Not only was she in the vast and despised minority as a Jew, but she was also a woman. And not only was she a woman, but a newly-crowned queen, succeeding someone who had been banished for resisting the current authority. Esther's reasons to stay silent are not only plausible, they're entirely valid. But as the story goes, Esther chooses to be bold, calling on her community to lift her up in prayer, which ultimately gives her the confidence to speak on behalf of the Jewish people. In the end, they are saved. To read the book of Esther is to face the notion that God can call us into hard and scary situations, for He knows His power and grace are enough.

Personally, the story of Esther moves me deeply because it challenges me. As a young black woman with no seminary qualifications or official creative writing credentials, I often feel unqualified to speak, write, or create in a confident manner. And yet, this small strong call to tell stories remains. Not simply to tell stories that are inspiring, however, but also to tell stories that are raw, painful, and redemptive.

My experience as a minority looks much different than Esther's, but it has not been void of challenges, and it certainly has not been void of hope. Through the story of Esther, I am reminded that stories like mine need to be told. Not because they are any more special, but because they reveal something intricate about the heart of God.

So, on a cold January morning, my senior year of college, I took a step of faith and confidence and spoke openly about my experience with race thus far and the hope Christ continues to set before me.

What I found after sharing is that when we choose to open our hands and speak up when Christ calls us to, He always undoubtedly shows up. My words were imperfect, but I am confident they were used for *such a time as this.*

Through the story of Esther, we are called to see a God who cares deeply about His children, calling them into places and spaces where His voice can be heard. Through the story of Esther, I am reminded that there is a "for such a time as this" moment within us all and it is a glorious and truly transformative thing to listen.

· *Where do you find yourself in the story of Esther?*
· *How might God have placed you for such a time as this?*

Cup 52 | Poured Out

"Mary therefore took a pound of expensive ointment made from pure nard, and anointed the feet of Jesus and wiped his feet with her hair. The house was filled with the fragrance of the perfume."

John 12:3 ESV

When I first contemplated the prospect of *52 Cups of Coffee*, I was thrilled by the potential of what it could become. Initially, I approached the task with a certain confidence. The project, still in its ideation, seemed simple, straightforward, and easily manageable, but as I began to edit, I found that God wanted more from me. More words. More depth. More vulnerability. This was a call for transformation.

I have often thought that books are written in coffee shops, or at the kitchen table in the early hours of the morning. This is true, I'm sure, but I'm also finding that the best writing – best as in most personally transformative – often occurs within the unexpected, and more times than not the inconvenient. Like at 2 am when you're beyond tired but can't seem to fall asleep – suddenly the words are spilling out and can't be contained. It is here that something sacred and inexplicably divine occurs, not asking for an explanation but obedience.

I wonder if Mary experienced this kind of divine spontaneity in John chapter 12. Was she simply minding her own business when out of the blue she felt compelled to take her most expensive oil and pour it on the feet of Jesus? It seems crazy when we think about it, doesn't it? Through earthly eyes, Mary's posture cannot quite be explained, but with spiritual eyes, her actions make perfect sense, for she was driven by the Spirit to act courageously as she demonstrated her commitment to God.

And this is where I find myself. For the past year, I have poured my heart into these stories, oftentimes not knowing where they were going or what they would become. As I poured, the Holy Spirit continuously opened my eyes and heart to the freedom that comes with reckless abandon at the feet of Christ.

I find a similar narrative in 2 Kings 4. As Elisha visits a woman in a desperate situation, he asks her for what she already has: one jar of oil. This woman is then sent out into her community to obtain more, and through that initial jar of oil, she is given a vessel to pour into all the others. God provided for her needs through what she already had. I believe the same is no less true of our own respective *jars*.

What I am finding is that the life of worship requires everything of us. It reaches into the deepest parts of our hearts and asks for all we've got, both when it's planned and when it's not. It's taking what we have and trusting God to use it beyond what we could do with it ourselves.

So, here we are. I'm not sure what will become of this collection, who will receive it or how they will respond, but here I am poured out and expectant, and I believe this is a particularly transformative place to be.

- *How has this collection of stories impacted the way you see God and the world?*
- *How can you share your own story today?*

Fifty-Two Cups of Coffee

A Final Note

I wonder if God wants to write a story in each of us. Maybe He wants to take the pen boldly to the blank page before Him. I wonder, however, if along the way we grab a pencil of our own, found in our desire for control and the perception that we have it. Do we then take that pencil and etch in miscellaneous details along with God's good handiwork in an attempt to alter or change the story in its entirety? Perhaps God sees our subtle and loud attempts and flashes a longing smile, a smile that encapsulates, *oh my child, if only you knew where I was going with that line.* But maybe He doesn't take the pencil from us, viciously erasing what we wrote. Maybe swiftly, gently, and all at once He continues to write a beautiful story amidst the things we have written, even amidst the character additions and plot development that we have tried to include on our own.

But what if we chose to drop our pencil and read the story God intended and continues to write. What if we chose to take a step back and trust the author of life, resting in and admiring each stroke of His pen, all the while in hopeful anticipation of where He will take it. What if we chose to simply read.

Thank You!

Within every story, there lies a community, and God has blessed me with an incredible one. Some I wrote about, most I did not. There is not nearly enough time or space to give credit to all the individuals who joined me in this journey, but I would be remiss if I did not specifically acknowledge the following people in the following ways.

To Mom and Dad – thank you for believing in me and this gift before I did. Dad, thank you for leading with both words and actions. I put God first because you taught me how. Mom, thank you for embodying everything I hope to become. I write because of you.

To my sisters, Natasha, Nicole, and Nadia – Natasha, thank you for teaching me to do everything with excellence. You truly inspire me daily. Nicole, thank you for challenging me to see the world in new ways and to always laugh along the way. Nadia, thank you for encouraging me to not take life too seriously. You remind me that discipline and adventure can co-exist.

To Uncle Phillip, Aunty Ruth, Crystal, Nicholas, and Nevaeh – thank you for making ordinary moments extraordinary experiences. Aunty Ruth, thank you for first encouraging me to write!

To Uncle Greg, Aunty Pat, and Matthew – thank you for loving me the way that you do. I am a better me when I'm with you.

To Grandma (Albina) – thank you for the numerous sacrifices you have made so that I could become the person I am today. You have taught me to follow my dreams.

To Grandma and Grandpa (Alpheus and Myrtle) – this book is rooted in the wisdom you have passed down for generations. Thank you!

To Ireana Cook – thank you for listening to my wild ideas and always offering an excited yet grounded "Yes, you can!" Your commitment to God and pursuit of excellence inspire me endlessly. Thank you for designing such a gorgeous book cover. You remind me that life is better when we do it together.

To the many people who looked at my drafts and shared their wisdom: Eugenia Ji, Maddie Walter, Sara Kimura, Pastor Randy York, Dr. Nina Bissett, Dr. Warren Anderson, Ms. Bobette Keasler. I cannot tell you thank you enough! You remind me why community is sacred.

To Mary Ellen Kettelhut– thank you for hearing my dream and telling me it was real. I am forever grateful for your wisdom and guidance.

To Katlyn Koegel – this book would not be here were it not for your *Thursday Emails* idea. Thank you for hearing the voice in me even when I could not hear it for myself.

To Ruth Demeke – I am still amazed by your character. Thank you for lending me your laptop when mine stopped working. I am forever blessed by your friendship.

To John Luke and the incredible community you rallied together to surprise with me a new laptop – I am still in awe. From the bottom of my heart, thank you.

To the friends whose names show up on these pages and those whose names do not, your wisdom not only inspires me but compels me to keep writing. Thank you!

And to you, the reader, I have spent most of this book writing process wishing that I could hear your story. I pray you find the courage to share it. Thank you for joining my community and thank you for reminding me of hope.

Finally, to God –I look forward to many more adventures with you. Thank you for entrusting me with something as sacred and special as this book. I am wholeheartedly convinced that you are the best there is.

With sincere gratitude,
Natalie Brown

References

Here
Chambers, Oswald. "The Sphere of Exaltation." *My Utmost for His Highest.* Discovery House, 2017.

Walking on Broken Glass
"Psalm 121." *ESV Student Study Bible: English Standard Version.* Crossway, 2011.

Meet Me at the Well
"John 4:6." *ESV Student Study Bible: English Standard Version.* Crossway, 2011.

Gifts of Desperation
Lamott, Anne. "Red Cords." *Plan B: Further Thoughts on Faith.* New York: Penguin Books, 2005.

Prayer of Patience
"Prayer of Teilhard de Chardin" Ingnationspirituality.com https://www.ignatianspirituality.com/8078/prayer-of-theilhard-de-chardin (accessed September 2016).

A Table in the Wilderness
Moen, Skip. "The Organized Life." Skipmoen.com. https://www.skipmoen.com/2008/04/the-organized-life/ (accessed May 2018)

Touching Heaven
"Dictionary of Bible Themes." BibleGateway.com https://www.biblegateway.com/resources/dictionary-of-bible-themes/5467-promises-divine (accessed September 2018)

Extra Notes!